HOW DO I KNOW?

A Paranormal Memoir

A. Wolfe

The Lovers (Temple Brother & Sister)

Cover Art by A. Wolfe

Cover Design by A. Wolfe

ISBN-13: 979-8-218-07470-8

FOR ALL OF MY READERS

My stories are true. The names of my characters have been changed to protect the privacy of everyone involved.

Dear Reader,

It's important for you to know that I call myself Diana throughout my memoir. You'll learn why later. My real last name appears twice.

The reason I'm sharing my paranormal experiences is to give you an idea of what it's like, how it feels, and what I've learned. Why me? Maybe it's because I ask for answers. This is the way of my life. I am the true child, student, experiencer, and experimenter in every story.

In our society, there is no early education for people with abilities like ours who want to understand reality. In the ancient temples, young girls and boys were paired and trained as equals. It's where I learned to be a protector.

Space is full of time and time is full of events. These can pop into the present, making you the observer. You never know what might show up when time gets out of line. If it can happen to me, it can happen to anyone. This is when reality can get weird.

A. Wolfe

San Rafael, California

October 31, 2022

ACKNOWLEDGMENTS

Thank you to my family and friends for expressing your creative spirit and sharing your music, art, and writing with me. I'm grateful to my inner family and friends for your behind the scenes contact. Your wise lessons encouraged me to think for myself about your inner world and our relationship to it as human beings.

To the invisible man who entered the rear passenger seat of my car, and advised me, saying, "Slow down," as I was about to speed around my favorite curve a little bit faster—thanks. I would have killed the motorcyclist who'd just wiped out there. I've been telling your story from my art studio, hoping to find someone else you've watched over. I know I'm not the only one.

Here's to acknowledging the influences of our beautiful natural world. Earth's communication loops makes it a tremendous and lively educator. Thanks to the helper creatures and to its machine reality for giving me a greater understanding of time. Dear readers—you'll see what I mean.

I appreciate everyone at the Artful Editor for working on my book project. I am grateful to your kind advisor, wonderful editors, the owner, and editorial manager for your expertise, communication skills, and guidance.

CONTENTS

1

HOW DO I KNOW I EXIST?

After our 2nd Friday Art Walk is over, a group of artists and staff decide to go out. It's getting dark when we step into the heart of downtown San Rafael, whose main streets remind visitors of Paris with their illuminated shop windows, streetlamps, and strings of lights overhead.

We agree on a busy Chinese restaurant that stays open late and offers music or comedy. Its street-front atrium and the low-lit, high-ceilinged main room are already filled with diners. We're lucky to be seated near the bar in a separate U-shaped lounge area with two modern leather couches, a couple of comfortable chairs, and tables strategically interspersed. It's perfect, almost like having our own private space in plain sight, and the nine of us pile in, taking it over.

Right away, we start talking about how the night went. During this popular event, the public can visit thirty-four individual art studios in our building. "See artists in their natural habitats like animals at the zoo," teases a staff member who overhears conversations while roaming the halls.

"Ha ha. Well, this wild creature had a good night," I say. "My secret icebreaker is telling visitors there's complete freedom of speech in this studio. Some people are intimidated by art just like math. Who knew?"

"The zoo came to *me*. A woman stripped naked just to try on one of my jackets." Ted, the new clothing designer whose studio is near mine, laughs. "I tried to shield her, but she told me that she couldn't care less. She had to see how it looked without any of the competing patterns she was wearing. I pulled the curtain closed because people were already ogling at the door." He throws his ringed hands up in the air and grins. "Well, what are you going to do?"

We have a good laugh and start making up additions to Ted's story while sipping on Kung Fu cosmos, speaking without any filters, the way artists can. One boisterous painter plops onto Ted's lap, so we're in an uproar when our waiter comes to the lounge wearing a smile. We rein in our giggles as he passes out menus. We're in the middle of deciding what dishes to share when a strange thing happens.

A man walks into the restaurant and announces, "I will buy a drink for anyone who can answer my question." A hush comes over the room.

What an odd offer. Diners wait quietly, and those drinking at the bar pause to look his way. So do we. No one moves. Maybe everyone is wondering if this is the night's comedy act.

How Do I Know?

The man surveys the room. After seeing that he has everyone's attention, he asks, "How do I know I exist?" When we artists hear his question, we're as silent as everybody else.

I wonder how many places he's asked this question tonight. *Is he serious?*

The stranger's question is still warming the air when the idea comes to me. My friends look surprised when I stand up. I give them a playful glance and make my way over to the man so that I'm the first in line to answer his weird question.

Before speaking, I turn around to see how many people are behind me. I'm puzzled to find there's no one else lined up. *Why not? Free drink.*

I glance at my friends again and see they're giving me curious looks. I already have a reputation for welcoming anyone who comes to my art studio. Some visitors just need something from another human being. They'll often start by asking what my art means, and they'll buy something as a memento when our conversation helps them. My friends don't know that my life has always been like that. "I'll talk to anything with a mouth that doesn't act like it wants to eat me for lunch," I've said, making them laugh.

Maybe the man standing in front of me needs an answer for a philosophy class? I note his longer haircut, casual jacket, and dark pants. He looks organized behind the eyes, and I don't spot signs of any deteriorating health issues.

Since I'm not speaking to the entire room, I face him and say, "I have the answer to your question." I use a gentle voice and serious tone in case any response to his question means the world to him.

He doesn't respond, so I connect by locking on to his blue eyes. To help with my delivery, I slow down, saying, "Through time and memory, and memory of a time before this time and this body—see?"

I wait and watch as the man considers my response. His expression doesn't reveal if he likes my answer or not, and he stares upward until his eyes slowly begin to flicker with understanding. That's when both of his hands dive into his pants pockets.

He starts digging. He digs and he digs, and I soon learn why. He not only wants to buy me a drink, but he also wants to buy one for everyone in our group.

"You don't have to do that. It wasn't part of the deal," I say, but he insists, telling me that he has enough money for all of us.

The stranger looks happy as he gives me a handful of cash. When I thank him, he nods and leaves the restaurant. I watch him disappear before heading to the bar.

"Nine Kung Fu cosmos for the lounge, please," I tell the bartender. Just like it had already been calculated, there's exactly enough cash for our drinks plus the tip.

When I take my seat back at the lounge, everyone wants to know what happened. I give my answer to the man's query. "That sounds kind of woo-woo," says Carol, a realist painter, looking puzzled.

"Yeah, it's way off your canvas," Ted teases her while winking at me.

The word *woo-woo* makes me grin and I say nothing more. My friends just haven't seen time get out of line. Time and space shifts can happen whether you're awake or asleep, and they can alter reality right in front of you in unbelievable ways, like magic.

My friends are surprised when our waiter shows up with a tray full of drinks. "From the stranger who liked my answer," I tell the cheering artists.

2

INSIDE-OUT CHILD

My first day on earth began on a winter afternoon according to the no-nonsense, no-exaggeration truth-teller with just a few spare-your-feelings white lies to her name: my mother. She was pregnant but not at full term.

This small-boned woman-with-child made twenty-five pounds look more like a fifty-pound load. Her belly was huge like a cage ball and even strangers asked if she was going to have twins.

After eating lunch at home with her family, my mother and father walked the few blocks to Good Hope Hospital. These two newlyweds barely made it up the steps to their destination—the labor, delivery, and recovery room.

A very short labor and easy birth made it a lucky Friday the thirteenth. The date was verified on the birth certificate, although the hospital neglected to clearly note a.m. or p.m. when recording the time.

How Do I Know?

It's hard to imagine being stuffed within a woman's belly for almost a year. Had I been in there all along, ferociously guarding my new body from all the other souls who wished to have my mother as their mother? Since I was a honeymoon baby and an early girl, she only had to pack me for about eight months.

Do we enter a womb on earth right at the time of conception, in the flash of an instant, like a lightning bolt finding some ground? I don't recall waiting or hovering above her before being whisked into a long, light-streaked tunnel and through her birth canal at the very last minute.

My newborn body—brain included—was healthy. My weight and measurements were normal, and I passed all the reflexive and neurological tests of the day.

Like a novelty, I was passed around to seven young adults, two grandparents, two godparents, and the ladies who worked in the large house owned by my mother's parents. "You were sunny and smiled a lot like your father, so none of us ignored you—our first child of the next generation," Mother told me when I was older. "You would lie in your crib, arms stretched toward the ceiling, staring at your hands for hours."

Maybe I appeared to be fixated on my new body when I was missing and reaching for the other world—still feeling more attached to it than the one I'd just landed in. This would excite me more than a physical pair of arms and hands. It must be why my baby limbs were often outstretched in a pick-me-up position.

Some things I couldn't forget, like entertaining patterns and flashes of light on the ceiling of Dad's car as we headed north. My sister was three months old. I was thirteen months ahead of her. We were moving away from our grandparents.

Remembering my life before the one in this body wasn't easy. Trying to hold on to it, to keep it in my mind, made perfect sense. If I could still see it, I'd find a way to get back in.

So, at age three, I created a place to enter it by twirling in deep, fresh snow. The earthly surroundings faded, whizzing into a circle created by my spinning. The atmosphere grew lighter. More white light appeared, glistening with countless specks of crystalline colors.

I turned around and around—right into a round, enchanted igloo world of perfect snow. Here, one edge of each tiny white flake had a shadow that bounced against part of another flake and transformed the darkness into brilliance, reflecting and sparkling with the entire spectrum of colors that can be seen in full sunlight.

"I'm in!" I shrieked when I got beyond dizzy. "I'm in my little white room." Being in all that altered beauty, I felt lighter than air. The weightlessness created feelings of pure joy.

My sister Helen was outside and close by. She watched, but she didn't call out or try to copy me. Maybe she didn't know what twirling could do. Or else she had forgotten.

My ambitions weren't earthbound, even as a toddler. I didn't want to be a human. Yes, I wanted to be an angel. No, I didn't blab it around. My desire to be an angel, like the desire to teach or take up any other chosen work, was one of my earliest secrets.

O

The next thing to stay quiet about comes soon after. I'm still three years old when a stranger visits me. This guest is an older boy who comes with a different kind of friendship.

He doesn't need to ring the front doorbell like a regular person because it almost seems like he lives in our house. One day, he just appears. Although he doesn't act like he's trying to hide from anyone, he is my secret.

For about a year, whenever my parents are busy or tending to my little sister, I sneak into the pantry to see my friend. Wood shelves stocked full of food line two sides of the storeroom, but there is nothing worth climbing up to get since I'm too young to cook.

Faded rose wallpaper covers the back wall in here. The light switch in this pantry is too high to reach, but with the door open, there's soft natural light. It isn't too bright to reveal our secret. The back of the pantry is where the boy and I meet—in the same place, at the same spot, where there is a large, odd stain on the wall. He only appears here.

I always bring a real soupspoon with me to feed him, dipping my big ladle right where he stands in front of that oval stain on the wall. Maybe he's told me that he's starving and that's why I bring such a large spoon. I talk while I feed him, and I stop when he speaks.

While I can't describe what he looks like, or even what we talk about, he is very light because my mother can't see him, and my father doesn't either. I don't think he's imaginary because it's not my style to hallucinate another human being or anything else.

What I do know is that he's real and his name is Worse-A-

Doodle. He's already in school and old enough to spell his unusual name. I can't read and only know exactly how he pronounces it.

If my parents hear our whispers coming from the pantry, they don't ask any questions, and they don't discourage my trips to the pantry or disrupt our friendship. I wonder now if I was too innocent to realize that he may have been a ghost? Or maybe he had a body somewhere and his spirit wandered over to our house.

This is the same year that I end up with the big holiday secret. After a storm, snowplows have gotten to work piling it up like barriers. Though many footsteps have leveled the snow, the sidewalks are still icy and white.

Our family is bundled up in winter clothes when we go downtown to see how all the shops are decorated for Christmas. Dad carries Helen while he walks arm in arm with my mother, whose free hand holds mine. We stop in front of a store window that has more toys than I've ever seen in one place.

My mother and I take our time to look at dolls on shelves that go up to the ceiling. When we've seen all of them, she bends down. She's at my height and pushes her dark brown hair behind an ear before moving her face closer to mine. In a low whisper, she asks, "Which doll do you like?"

What an odd question. As I stare into her hazel eyes, I am suspicious.

Why are you asking me if Santa is supposed to bring me a doll? I just look at her red lipstick and decide there's no way I'm going to say what I'm thinking about Santa.

I give my mother a sideways look and point to the most beautiful doll—even touching the glass in front of her. She stands out because she's different from all the other dolls, and that's why I want her. We don't go in because the store is already closed.

Thanks to the Advent calendar, every day leading up to Christmas Eve seems long. Finally, Christmas Day rolls around and all of us head down the stairs to our decorated living room.

When Mother turns on the tree lights, I get a surprise. My new doll is under the tree. She's the right doll but the wrong color, and that gives everything away. Santa wouldn't have brought me this doll. Santa would have given me the black doll that I wanted.

Now I know there's no Santa. My parents are acting as Santa because they've gotten this doll. She's how I figure out there's no such thing as Santa Claus.

Even though I'm only three, the last thing I want to do is spoil Christmas for my parents. My sister still believes in Santa Claus, so I won't ruin her day either. I try to hide my disappointment when looking at the doll.

Secrets to keep seem to come one after the other—three of them for my three years of age. These realizations and experiences are small, but they are like milestones and make unforgettable impressions on me. I'm only a toddler, but I can put some patterns together.

O

It's now spring in our new home, a world away from relatives, so I find a nice elderly couple to adopt who live two townhouses away. I give them flowers that I just picked from the yard of a crabby old woman who yells at me.

I make my way back to where Mother stands with our front door open. I head inside and go upstairs while she and my sister stay downstairs.

I love the feeling of flying. That's why I like to stand on the long arms of the rocking chair to rock back and forth, using it as a springboard to dive onto the bed. But if I do, Mother will hear me since the house is quiet. She'll run to my bedroom and put a stop to it immediately. So, although I'm a daredevil, I'm upstairs behaving myself.

I'm enjoying doodling in a coloring book. It has my attention. I'm happy to have the room to myself without the distractions of my younger sister. I choose the crayon colors, and then scribbling is the main sound in the room. I'm busy filling the cartoon characters and scenery with color. My ears are tuned to the stairs in case I have to grab my materials before my sister comes this way.

The sounds of voices in conversation are coming from someplace. This doesn't concern me because nobody's talking to me. I keep coloring. The fun of deciding which color to use for the hair and what crayon to choose for the shoes shifts my focus back to what's in front of me. I scribble in the hair with the brown crayon that's closest to my mother's color.

The voices of men and women sound like they are coming closer. There's a window cracked open because it's warmer now, and a breeze must be carrying the voices of our neighbors outside on their porches.

It's just background noise until I realize people are trying to get my attention. I don't look up. I just listen casually as I color. These adult voices *are* talking to me.

Me? Talking to me? Why? They are not only talking to me—they are talking about me, to me. It's kind of like being in the pantry with my friend Worse-A-Doodle, who hasn't visited me lately. I listen for him, but I don't hear him in the crowd.

Finally, I look up in the direction of these voices. When I do, they come even closer. Now they know I can hear them, and that's when they really start talking.

After finding out the truth about Santa Claus, I don't know what to think of adults. I wonder why Worse-A-Doodle isn't with these visitors if they also live in the house.

"Just because I'm only four doesn't mean I'm going to believe everything you tell me," I let them know.

Then I walk to the bathroom and shut the door. I look down at the print on my clothes and think about what the voices have said. The group doesn't follow me. I think about who they are and decide they must be older relatives. I make my decision. I'll listen, but they'll have to prove themselves before I believe them.

When I come back to the bedroom, the group is already in agreement. They have more to say. "Do not tell anybody about us. People are going to come looking for you."

Their tone is serious. It is something about their tone that impresses me, and I decide to abide by their wishes. I don't talk to anyone about them. But I don't understand why people will come looking for me. *Me? What would be the point of that?*

O

From that day on, I'm an observer. No one in my family talks about the people who visit sometimes. I don't think that I'm special at all, but I am different for some reason.

As the days unfold, what these strange visitors have said about my immediate future turns into my reality. This proves they've told me the truth. Now, I trust them. They are good people.

This is one of the biggest secrets I've ever had to keep. Yes, I'm learning that I'm different. I hide it and never reveal this part of myself so I can live a normal life. If I live a normal life, the people who are looking for me will never find me. This is how my young mind takes their message—as a warning to be careful here.

By age five, I decide this world must be dead. *Where's the life?* I wonder. *Is something just missing in people?* I love and enjoy people, except for that witch neighbor who yells at me for picking flowers.

I don't know how to describe what I'm seeing. People just look kind of dead, like my doll. This isn't meant to be an insult. I just don't know how to say it at my age.

3

EXTRACURRICULAR ACTIVITIES IN CHURCH

My eyes opened like I'd just blinked and found myself there, trance-staring straight ahead. No breezes blew, so my escape-artist hair stayed put somehow instead of slipping out to tickle my face. I didn't feel the weight of my body because my bare feet weren't touching anything. This didn't disturb me.

It felt relaxing to stand upright and float without falling over. With no need for treading, both arms were at rest, dangling down with my palms and fingertips lightly touching my thighs.

There was a sense—as though the blackness had been there all along. It was the vast blackness of space, and I was a little elementary school girl.

How had I reached this destination? It didn't bother me that I didn't know. *Maybe we all come here and just don't remember it,* I thought.

Things changed when random shapes and textured shards came into view. They flew in from every direction—colorful pieces of bright beauty breaking up the darkness to form a breathtaking globe on a background of night.

This display of creation was something to behold, but the structure itself wasn't built to last. The intricate sphere exploded into countless pieces that went flying out of existence or maybe back to an original source. There were no reactive waves from its eruption, and no noisy echoes disturbed the stillness. The endless velvet black space was in front of me again and nothing else.

I observed this curious event without feeling alarmed or having any emotion. I didn't even shift my position.

The silence was broken when a male voice requested, "Now you do it." Sounding wise, experienced, and matter of fact, the man wasn't ordering or pushing me to do what he'd done. Although I couldn't see him, I wasn't frightened. I knew he was speaking to me because no one else was around.

I didn't reply to the man's request, and he didn't demand any response from me. Everything was silent—just as it was in the beginning. But the endless space was now a classroom, and its perfect darkness was like a clean blackboard. The invisible man wasn't like any person or teacher I'd ever met.

How did I know what to do on my own? I don't have the answer. Somehow, I knew and just did it.

How Do I Know?

When colorful patterns and designs appeared like magic, they were lit like sunlight coming through a kaleidoscope or stained glass. My arms were still at my side. It was the strangest thing—my fingers weren't needed for this task. I used my mind to bring an orb into being and watched as my thoughts caused the pieces to organize themselves. My construction was more complex than a microchip and as detailed as a half-million-piece puzzle or a mandala. It was like building a world.

I admired my sphere floating in space. It was beautiful and now it was complete. Then came some thoughts.

I'm just a little girl. This invisible man is the expert. It would be arrogant to think that I could make a complicated object as well as he did.

Without asking for permission, I exploded my creation. It was like shattering a crystal globe back into black space. I started over. In flew parts and sections. This time, the shape was not a perfect circle. Pieces flew in and rejected parts flew out as I built and rebuilt it a few more times. The newest areas looked wobbly and too geometrically incorrect to keep, so in frustration, I blasted it all back to black with a sad-eyed blink.

With that last blink, I was startled to feel my cheeks wet with tears. I sensed the weight of being back in bed and settling in my body as I cried over my creation, worrying that I'd just done something awful.

Turning my head from side to side caused the spilling tears to zigzag. Some oozed into the corners of my blubbering mouth until their seawater flavor and the sound of someone speaking distracted me.

"It's all right, Diana. You did it right the first time," the man assured me.

This invisible teacher heard my thoughts. How else could he answer me?

Because I didn't expect to hear him when I wasn't in black space, the clearness of his message astonished me. I felt my heart's heaviness begin shifting away from the unfamiliar dragging despair that was shaking me. Just ten words from him erased the doubt and burden of my task.

I began my habitual review of events and my actions, as though this had happened to someone else. I didn't question whether I'd been in space. Being in space was familiar to me, but being given the responsibility to create there was something new.

Yes, the man knew my name without asking. Am I supposed to know him? He doesn't sound like someone I wouldn't want to know. But I would have recalled meeting him since I'm the kind of girl who remembers everything.

This was my thinking, and it went around a few times. The anonymous man with his dream lesson was an experience I wouldn't mention to anyone. After making this decision, it was easier to let everything about it go. After a long exhale, I dozed off.

The next time my eyes opened, it was morning. Back was my sunny, positive self—my normal face.

O

How Do I Know?

At midday, our mother gives a two-note whistle, signaling that it's time for lunch. We come running, and the cat that has adopted our family takes up the rear in the race to our house. He waits outside while we run inside and head to the kitchen table.

My sisters and I eat—more like we inhale our lunch without much chatter. Right after, Helen and Chase bound down the hall and out the front door. I stall, hoping my sisters won't notice that I'm not right behind them.

Mother nods her approval at the objects I slide out of hiding. "Keep it up," she whispers. I wave and leave through the kitchen door, ducking along the back of the house and clutching the books I'd been sitting on. This bookworm is a sought-after girl. I have too much fun having fun. Invitations and requests to play come daily from my sisters and friends. Dance parties happen on the weekends, and that's when all five members of our Love Club go, including me. But right now I must hide—just to have more time to read.

The uneven roughness of the house's stone exterior delivers poking jabs to my spine. I flatten myself against its discomfort anyway, watching and waiting.

A total peacefulness surrounds the backyard, as though all of nature is resting in unison. I breathe in the fragrant honeysuckle and marvel at the thick canopy of healthy summer foliage. It hides many large limbs of a giant maple tree at the end of our property. Within this tree's deepest green shades, where the temperature is cooler, is a perfect place to read. Secretly, it's my maple tree since no one else has claimed it.

Rarely does anyone climb this tricky tree requiring longer legs and bravery. The spaces and layers between its branches allow glittering splashes of sunlight to adorn it. I love this healthy tree and put it on a pedestal.

All is quiet within a dense row of trees lining one side of the church next door, where children like to play hide-and-seek. Our screened porch is shaded by these tall dark pines. This peace can change any second, and if it does, I might be the one who needs to hide there in a hurry.

Only the watchful eye of nature knows I'm here. It is invisible and observes me from the backyard, where those scratchy pines separate our home from the church and its creed.

To read by day without interruption, I sneak off somewhere. Nobody knows about my love of reading except for the librarians, my parents, and now my teachers. Each new school year, we have to list the books we've read over the summer. To keep my secret, I turned my two-page list of books over when passing it forward at the start of class. Luckily, the teacher was the one to flip it faceup.

Snapping to attention, I find myself standing with a book of illustrated fairytales that I've already read—renewed at the library this time for its beautiful, detailed art. The other book is a random discovery.

Greek mythology? Like fairytales? I had scanned the first two pages of Cupid and Psyche's love story and the last paragraph before leaving the library, to make sure it wasn't a dud.

What a find. Fantastic and so intriguing that even the art could wait a minute. As I learn more of these tales, I realize I may never look at anything the same way again—especially nature itself.

Mother's head probably isn't in the kitchen window just yet—she is a slow and mannered eater. We girls are lucky that we don't have to wait for her to finish eating before running for our childhood, which both parents want us to enjoy. It is so brief a time, they've told us, though it feels like a long time to me.

I blow my breath out and try sucking in my full stomach, hoping this will help create more space. Having slender arms and long legs may be an advantage for climbing trees, but it doesn't help right after eating. After cramming the giant fairytale book into my shorts, I squish and squeeze until the smaller book is finally on top.

Dashing across the yard, I hug myself to keep the shifting books from popping out of my shorts. They bump against my ribs as I make my way to the maple tree. I place one fast-moving foot into a large hollow area of the trunk to get a jump up to the next cavity. It's high, and the books give me a jabbing reminder when I get to the first branch.

After corralling roaming strands of baby-fine hair behind each ear, I hoist myself up. Once I'm past the danger of standing on my toes to reach the next branch, I climb higher to find a comfortable reclining bough that isn't visible to anyone.

That's when the stealthy eye of nature springs into action. It's uncanny how our adopted cat shows up whenever I decide to read in this tree. He doesn't follow anyone else. He has a graceful appearance, his gray-and-black tiger stripes in motion as he lets me lead the way and climbs up behind me. After I pick my branch, he chooses the branch across from it. I read while my four-legged friend naps.

It isn't long before squeals and laughter make their way into the backyard. I get a top view of Helen's head, her hair parted to one side. I spot Chase's sun-streaked middle part as they search for me.

"Diana, Diana." Chase calls my name sweetly. "I put my pet locust back so it can go home," she chirps. Yesterday she surprised the family by wearing a live locust like a piece of jewelry and then walking around with it on her nose. What a weirdo.

Helen's voice is impatient and demanding. "Diana. Diana. Di-an-a, where are you?" She turns in every direction in case I'm sneaking up on her again. Helen doesn't forget anything either. "Uh-huh, I know you're around." Her hunch is good too. She crosses her arms like our coach Dad, then flaps them against her ribcage while yelling my name again. "Di-an-a!"

This sister never accepts that I can't always put her first or go along with whatever she wants. Today I want to read more than play. I love her, but I'm not a yes girl. Our relationship is difficult and becomes a battle of wills whenever we aren't in agreement.

Little Chase waves her solid arms in the air like a conductor's. "Oh, Diana. Oh, Diana," she sings. "Come out and play." She isn't giving up easily.

The cat looks at me and blinks like he knows my name when he hears it. *Does he really?* Just in case he does, I copy his rhythm and give him a blink back. We lower our heads in unison to watch my sisters crisscross left and right as they search the backyard. They disappear behind the house and run back around again with even redder faces.

Then they stop directly beneath my huge maple tree to cool off in its shade. Chase grabs her bangs and holds them tightly to keep them off her face. Helen pulls at her shirt like she's fanning herself with it. They're both quiet.

Now, the cat and I have become part of the invisible eye of nature. I can't believe they don't see us. Maybe it's because the clothes I'm wearing blend in with the large tree limb. My sisters give up and run off. When the echoes of my name fade out and our backyard is quiet again, the tiger cat and I look at each other. As soon as he closes his eyes, I return to my book.

No one ever found out about my favorite reading hideaway, and I never mentioned my secret companion who followed me there. It's my good fortune that no one ever thought to look up.

O

Time zips by when unconstrained by four school walls. It's summer and it's good to be free. I take my bike on side streets early, baring my teeth when coasting near two white standard poodles observing me from the large corner window of their gray cedar shake home. These statue-perfect canines are groomed like show dogs. Even though the pair don't bark and aren't moved by my display of fangs, I know they're real because I've seen them stand up.

Loud, birdlike calls of "Flick, flick, flick, flick, fickle!" come from a fenced-in yard. They're uttered by an older girl who used to model but then had a breakdown. She lives with her parents now and maybe forever. I've yelled hello and she has talked back, but it's never long before she gets stuck and repeats these *flick* words again like she's a broken doll.

I speed past single-story brick houses, leafy trees, green yards, two-story wood homes, and a tree-lined dirt lane with grass, pebbles, and weeds growing in the middle of tire tracks that go on a long way— maybe about a quarter mile. I end up at an old abandoned historical mansion, slowing down by the mortuary, which I've already been inside. It showed me what death looks like on a young girl about my age. She was killed on a nice Sunday drive with her family when she decided to lay her head on the back passenger seat armrest. Their car collided with a large truck that smashed its way inside where she was sleeping. I walked into the viewing room to pay my respects to a stranger, and I saw her in an open coffin. I wanted to learn what I could about death just in case I should die when I reached her age too. No one knows when their time will come.

I brake for dead animals and slow my roll just enough to take my feet off the pedals. I stand still in front of a big taxidermy shop window to see if anything new has been stuffed and preserved for its beauty forever. I admire the poses of birds, raccoons, squirrels, antler-headed bucks, and I wonder if the same people own the mortuary since the shops are close to each other. I think about a gray cat that died in some tall weeds right off the path not too far from my house. I can't tell how it died and I don't want to touch it. The dead spot is close enough to return to every few days to check the progress of decay. The maggots are gone and its body is too dried out to reek. I want to know how much time it will take for the cat to look like a skeleton.

How Do I Know?

The turn to Ty's house is coming up. I take a sharp left, going off
the road to a hard, level path full of long-branched willow trees, more
green yards, and fences with overhanging honeysuckle, wisteria, and
lilac bushes. I roll my bike onto blades of wet grass as I head into the
yard of my favorite boyfriend for games and swimming.

"Hi, gorgeous. We have enough players to make it a volleyball
game now," says Ty. "We can swim right after that." Ty's dark brown
hair shines in the sunlight. He's a smart and cute boy in our class, and
we're in the fastest reading group.

I raise my hand to brush wisps of hair aside like the breeze that
blew them there. As I shield my eyes to look at him, my emerald
costume ring glints in the full sun. Ty likes to surprise me with jewelry.
Both Ty and Bill give jewelry to Relia, Chloe, and me. I've heard that
boys aren't supposed to like girls at our age, but that's not true in our
world.

"You know how much I love to play volleyball. Thanks for
inviting me. See? I'm wearing the ring you gave me."

Ty nods and says, "I noticed." His hands go into his pockets as
he leans toward me so that our heads are almost touching. "I see you
don't need to bite off all of your fingernails before we play," he teases,
knowing I will put sports before long nails. Ty straightens back up and
stretches his arms above his head.

"Biting them off at the same time is how I quit. Might as well get
it over with all at once for a real reason," I say. Now Ty knows that's the
way I quit chewing on them. I smile at him as I take the ring off and put
it in my bag. "Relia and Chloe want me to ask if you and Bill want to go

for a hike with us on Thursday afternoon. We'll meet at Chloe's first. After that, we'll go to Relia's house to finish looking at those gross photos in her mom's medical books."

"Sure. Bill liked seeing them too—we'll ask him." Ty gives me a warm look with those confident brown eyes. This starts our game— speaking with our eyes. He stares into mine and I feel my cheeks and neck flush with warmth. I ignore my blushing and look right back at him. We're locked in with our eyes now and Ty moves a bit closer. I admire his tan and the fit of his T-shirt and notice that we're still about the same height. I try to think about the fun of being in the reading group with him and not the way his nose looks funny when it's right in my face. The closer he gets, the funnier this becomes. I take a half step closer, determined not to break my gaze, and I work to disrupt his concentration with eye rolls and lash flutters right against his face. He grins. When I see nothing but his teeth, I can't hold in a giggle, so that breaks the link.

I don't know why Ty and I do this to tease each other, but we do. We have an easy friendship, and he's like the brother that I don't have but wish I did. It's why I love hanging out with boys.

At Ty's, it's just like playing ball with boys in school. I know what to expect, always being the only girl. Ty is a captain just like his dad. He and the other team's leader toss a coin to see who gets to choose the first player. Ty picks his best friend first out of loyalty, and that's Bill—my other boyfriend. I understand why. Ty will pick me next over the other boys because he knows that I can play better and help us win. He does. I notice the looks the other boys give—they don't understand this, and I don't know that I'm not supposed to win because I'm a girl.

How Do I Know?

We play and I get most of the action, but I'm not the weak spot. Ty knows it. He grins and whispers in my ear, "You're the secret weapon."

Is this why Ty and Bill give me jewelry? No. They also give rings to my two best girlfriends, Relia and Chloe, who don't play sports with the boys.

We swim after, and then straight from the pool, I put my clothes on over my wet swimsuit. I hear about the next game and leave, then speed dry in the breeze, taking straighter concrete sidewalks and an asphalt route to meet Relia and Chloe. They'll want to know all about today since we share our boyfriends—who are almost like our girlfriends.

Chloe's single-story brick home with black shuttered windows and a double door sits at the top of a sloping green hill shaded by trees. I spot two faces—Chloe's, with her short dark brown sweep of hair, and Relia's, surrounded by beautiful blond ringlets that her mother curls every day.

Chloe and Relia greet me at the front door with Mary right behind them. She's the maid, and she's in charge because she's the only adult in Chloe's house. Chloe, Relia, and I like to sit and eat with her because she's a funny and wise lady who answers our questions and laughs with us. We girls begin where we left off, and Mary listens to us talk about our lives like another friend. She gets Cokes from the fridge and sits back down with us. We tell jokes and finish our drinks, but I notice that I'm still thirsty, so I switch to water after that.

We manage to get away from our Chloe's bossy older sister and a sister too young for our conversations by running down the hall and locking Chloe's bedroom door. Relia and I lean against either side of the four-poster bed, and Chloe sits down in the middle. I tell them what I couldn't say in front of Mary—club's rules.

"Ty and Bill are both coming over on Thursday."

Chloe and Relia clasp hands and hop up and down with the news. Relia's ringlets fly like coiled ribbons. Then they each take one of my hands and we circle around chanting, "Love Club, Love Club, Love Club—shh."

Relia checks her pockets like she's forgotten something. "Mom has another medical book she thinks we'll want to see," she says. "Found it." She hands me a wadded-up gold chain with a butterfly pendant. "I've already looked at a few photos. Ew. You won't believe it."

"I would," Chloe says, sorting through a pink jewelry box. She pulls out two chain necklaces that are tangled together beyond return. "I can't wait to go hiking. I have an idea. We can see a movie next time. It'll be like we're back in the coat closet at school."

"Ha ha. We've had some fun in there. Relia, who do you like best—Ty or Bill?" I ask while gently rolling her twisted necklace with my fingers to get the kinks out.

"I like both of them the same," she replies sincerely. She twirls a ringlet around her forefinger while watching me work. "What about you, Chloe?" Relia's blue eyes sparkle as she stands on one leg with her hand holding the bedpost like a ballerina.

Before Chloe can answer, Relia includes me in a pledge, saying,

"We promise we won't tell." I nod at Chloe in agreement.

Chloe stops fishing around in her jewelry box and fixes her brown eyes on us, her long lashes fluttering. Accepting our pledge, she announces, "I believe you." With a serious look, she places her right hand with its pink nail polish over her heart and whispers, "That's why nobody's found out about our Love Club." Then she answers Relia's question. "It's hard to choose because I like them both."

After sorting through everything in her jewelry box, Chloe ends up handing me her biggest jumble—those two tangled necklaces. "What about you, Diana?"

"I bite. Me too," I say, sticking my tongue out. "Well?" It's not easy to say with my tongue clamped by my teeth.

Relia's and Chloe's eyes bug out when they try to talk this way. They sound crazy. We can barely understand each other, but we keep this up until our eyes drip tears and our mouths drool. That's when we decide to play a game of who can come up with the funniest sentence.

We're in a state of heaving laughter, and I'm trying my best to keep untangling the necklaces that their patience has given up on. Chloe hands out tissues just before the drool gets everywhere.

When we've finally calmed down enough, I finish by saying, "See how easy?" Chloe and Relia give each other looks. I've untangled the chains they've threatened to throw away, and they're both happy that I talked them out it.

"You don't give up," Chloe says admiringly.

"Both of you helped because I can do it when we talk."

We head outside to talk about meeting Ty and Bill in Chloe's yard. It'll be here under this tree on Thursday. "They won't have to knock on the door," says Chloe. "I'll tell Mary. She'll keep it quiet so my little sister won't know our plans and follow us."

It's time to go, and there's no beating the feeling of the sun's rays soaking into my skin. When coasting, I let go of the handlebars to give the sweat beading on my forehead a sideways swipe with the back of my hand. By the time I get home, my shirt is damp and sticking to me.

My throat—parched from the heat—feels as dry as a waterless wasteland looks. I race through the back door and straight to the kitchen to pour myself a drink. The room is shady and cool, and the café-curtained windows are the eye-catching bright spot without any angled sunlight breaking in.

I check to see how camouflaged my maple tree hideaway is from the sink at the window. *Good, like disappearing into the middle of a thick boxwood shrub.*

My eyes travel slowly beyond the window valence and higher up the kitchen wall, passing the wood trim molding, and when I get to the ceiling light in the middle of the room, I've tipped my head back enough to drink the entire glass of water in one continuous gulp.

This glimpse of the ceiling triggers the memory of looking down into a handheld mirror while walking around the house. I recall that my five-year-old self found it entertaining to do because it really looked like I was walking on the ceiling and would trip if I didn't step over the tops of doorframes and lighting fixtures.

I refill my glass of refreshing water and guzzle it with eyes closed to replay some of the silly actions of my littler self. As I tilt my head to face the ceiling again, some water splashes down my chin and throat. I don't mind.

As my body cools down, I notice a subtle change. The way the water is filling me up starts to feel unusual. It isn't easy to describe being underwater and above water at the same time or how the atmosphere in the room has changed. The kitchen now has that fuller feeling of both closeness and expansion, which doesn't make sense because there's no one here except me.

I try giving myself a possible explanation. *Maybe I'm feeling this way because the house is too quiet, like nobody's home.* It's rare to be alone here, but I am. This may be so, but my sonar tells me that people are standing close by. It's not a smothering sensation of being constricted and crowded by them—just a nice comforting feeling of good people being around.

While I'm having an internal-external yes-no debate, in comes an intuition of being guided. Yes, I'm a curious girl, so I follow it out of the kitchen and into the bathroom. The hand of invisible guidance stops its gentle pushes on my back right here, so here's where I decide to stay.

I flip the light switch and stand in front of the mirror. Although I am growing taller, I'm not checking my height to see if it's changed since yesterday, and I'm not taking a superficial look. I already know what my sweaty, rose-flushed face and damp hair look like after biking on a hot and humid afternoon.

Following a whim, I have a seat and look at my eyes. And I don't move or look away. I keep staring into them without blinking. The sight of a sudden, unexpected swirling cloud surprises me, but I don't blink. This growing cloud covers my reflection as it fills the mirror, and now my image is gone. Still, I don't blink.

Within the continuous motion of the cloud, something else comes to the surface and appears in the mirror. It's the face of a young woman whose features are different from mine, with darker skin and eyes. She's now the one reflected in the mirror and my image is gone.

I remain still as the first woman disappears and a second new face follows. She also has brown eyes, black hair, and dark skin.

Then, the next female appears, and another female takes her place—each image staying only for a few seconds, like a Queen of Diamonds card being placed exactly above the Queen of Hearts card. I see a few young girls around my age—then teenagers, one male, grandmothers, and women who could be mothers. The single image of a human skull appears, followed by more women.

Not the Jolly Roger—a regular human skull. How many people— thirty or more?

The faces and skull do not appear in any chronological order. Not one person has white skin, blond hair, and blue eyes—only me.

Now my eyes have that tired and uncomfortable feeling from staying open too long without blinking. When I finally do blink, the images disappear along with the cloud, and I reappear in the mirror as though nothing happened. I look the same—just about sixty seconds older, if that's an actual look.

My mind goes on its rounds looking for answers as I sit there. None come.

This is the weirdest experience yet. It's entertaining, so I know I'll try it again. I don't understand what it means, but part of me knows it isn't just play. No invisible teacher asked me to stare into a mirror without blinking this time, but it's another one of those unexpected lessons. These strange things—I just take them in stride. It doesn't bother me that I've been asked to hide this part of myself from everybody. I can be an irregular girl and still have fun.

O

Summer vacation is every day, but not this year. Mother has called for a family meeting in the living room. She's already seated at her piano when Helen and I arrive. Then Dad walks in carrying a cup of coffee with the sports page tucked under his arm. He's in a sunny mood as usual and wearing his coaching clothes—white T-shirt, shorts, shoes, and striped sport socks. His bright blue eyes crinkle when he blows us kisses. He sits in a recliner next to the fireplace. Helen and I have each chosen an arm of the sofa. Chase comes in last wearing socks and carrying her shoes. She plops down on the floor right in front of us, leans back, and begins to lace her sneakers.

This is the day my sisters and I get the news. "Girls. We think it's time for you to start going to church." *We? Church? Why?* I know it's Mother's new idea when we get a history lesson. "Our family first came to this country for freedom of religion," she says.

Then we should have the freedom to choose to go or not. Of course, I don't say this aloud. *Why is it so important that we must go to church now? Is Mother religious?* No one asks and I'm not about to either.

We know Mother had been her church's organist when she was a young girl. She's a talented musician. She reads the sheet music, but she doesn't need to because she has the true gift of playing by ear—following right along even if she's never heard the piece before. When she practices or plays her piano for us, it isn't church music she's playing—we know that for sure.

Are my sisters enthusiastic about going to church? I slyly eyeball Helen. She's slouching on the sofa and staring at me, her mouth a tight, unhappy slit. This usually means she's not pleased. Helen looks at me as if it's my fault or I must know something about why we have to go. I give her a hard, wide-eyed frown until she says, "What?"

When Mother looks at me, I don't answer Helen. I shrug and try my best to hide my thoughts about having to go to church for now. "Knock it off," I mouth to Helen. Then I stand up and announce, "I'm thirsty."

I pass by Chase on my way to the kitchen. She's fiddling with her new shoelaces as though she's not paying any attention and doesn't care. Her head is down and her shoulder-length hair is in her face, so I can't see her expression.

Dad peeks over the sports page. He runs a hand through his platinum hair and glances at me without saying anything. I get the feeling he would rather find a Sunday ball game, but I don't ask him. I already know our parents will stick together as a single unit once a decision has been made by either of them.

Going to church is something new, but in all honesty, I would rather be anywhere else. If we could vote on it as a family, our mother would be the only one attending church services—I'm sure of it.

We can't even pretend to forget it's Sunday to help us get out of going. The church has external speakers that broadcast the organist live. The musician's song choice can be heard blocks away. So, we have a kind of Sunday rooster alarm clock next door.

The Sunday music we've heard so far is not interesting. What our mother plays for us at home is much better. Those blaring church melodies have no catchy beats to entice us to sing or even dance. Having them blasted at us every week whether we like it or not only reminds me that now we'll have no choice in what we hear *or* where we go every Sunday.

O

The day comes too soon. "I'm dressed but not ready to go," I whisper. "See this?" I point to the three rows of money that our parents left for the offering plate. I pick mine up and put it in my purse.

Helen eyes the money. "I think I'll save mine to buy some candy. No one will know if I don't put it in the offering plate." With that remark comes her watchful stare. I know her routine. She wants me to say something so she knows where I stand. When I don't, she gets impatient and asks with a huff, "You're not going to tell on me, are you?"

While her comments surprise me, her question doesn't. "You don't want to go either. Okay, what's this? Turn around." Although I haven't answered Helen's question, she doesn't repeat it.

She shakes her head and hums a song we both like, making it harder to get the barrette out of her hair. She improvises by coming up with her own lyrics. "No, uh. I'm not excited, uh-huh at all about ugh, going to church."

I pick up where she leaves off. "Me ugh, either. Uh-huh. Finally, it looks uh-huh good."

"I bet we won't be singing this one in church," she says, and we both giggle.

Helen sure is fidgety. I don't mention her plan to buy candy as a possible reason. "Thanks," she says, slinging her purse over one shoulder.

We stand still in the hallway and wait, but not for long. I give her a mischievous look, hike up my dress, and do a few kicks. Helen follows right along with some exaggerated steps. We sing and dance until we hear footsteps heading to the top of the stairs.

Mother has helped Chase pick out a dress and she's ready to go. "When the offering plate is handed to you, put your money in and then pass it to the next person. Just watch Diana or Helen," Mother explains as she puts the money in her youngest child's purse.

Chase rubs her eyes and nods. She reminds me of a tulip in her flowered dress, slowly opening.

"Off you go. Thanks for being good girls." One by one, Mother bustles us out the door. There's no way to escape. She's smiling at us like this new experience is going to be the best thing ever.

So off we go, just a twenty-second walk away. *I guess Mother's working on getting Dad to go with her. He loves her so much that he'll go if it means that much to her.*

We're turning the corner when Helen says, "Look," and points to the living room window. "Mother's watching."

"Let's wave," says Chase. To please our little sister, we do.

O

The following Sunday, we sisters walk out of the church after hearing our second sermon. Chase asks, "Does Santa go to Jesus's house?" Helen and I do a double take.

Chase is serious. She studies my face while I try not to laugh. What a question.

Helen winks at me. "Go ask Mother. She probably knows."

We hear music as we get closer to the door. "Wait until she's finished playing," I say as Chase heads for the living room.

Helen grabs my arm and gives me a weird look. "Let's stand over here." She motions to some bushes before closing the front door. "When did you find out about Santa?"

It's still a sore spot with her. Helen believed in Santa until she was six years old. When her classmates told her that he wasn't real, she thought they were lying to her. Helen was so mad because I'd never told her that our parents were Santa.

"When we lived in Pennsylvania," I answer truthfully. I know she's embarrassed about not figuring it out, so I'm going to be careful not to rub it in.

Helen isn't satisfied. "How did you know?"

"This is how. Dad, Mother, you, and I went downtown to see Christmas decorations and a store window full of dolls."

"Didn't I get a doll too? Why didn't I know?" Helen interrupts.

"Yes, you got a doll." I smile at her question and reassure her. "You wouldn't be left out, but you weren't even two years old. That's why you don't remember." I tell her about the doll I wanted in the window and the doll that was under the tree instead.

"And that's how you knew there was no Santa? I don't get it." Helen's mouth starts getting that pout.

"Well, I didn't know there was no Santa until Christmas Day," I say.

"But you got the doll you wanted. You said you pointed to it. I still don't get it." Helen is getting worked up all over again.

She and I are already competitive enough, so I make sure it sounds like I haven't won anything. "I got the same doll, but it was white instead of black, and that's when I knew Mother and Dad were Santa."

"Okay. I get it now. The real Santa would have given you the black doll that you wanted." Helen's smile is back.

"That's it, smarty. I didn't want to spoil Christmas for everyone. So, I never told anyone that I knew." *And I didn't tell you because I knew that you were too young to understand.*

Helen kicks at the sidewalk in her fancy shoes like she's scraping off her grudge. Then she asks, "What about church? Do you think church is just make-believe like Santa?"

"Something's not right about it. Church seems to have a lot of made-up stuff like Santa to me. I don't even know why we have to go. It's not like what we're learning in school," I say, knowing Helen isn't going to blab my opinions about church.

"Why do you think Mother believes in God?" Helen asks a tough question.

"I don't know. Maybe because she can't believe in Santa— because he's not real?"

"God is her Santa," blurts Helen.

Maybe Helen has finally let go of the way she found out about Santa. Well, she learned to tie her shoes first because she and Mother are right-handed.

I try to make Helen feel better by saying, "Well, it's a right-handed shoe-tying world." She gets it. Now she can smile at me. When we're through giggling, I open the front door and wonder what we're going to be walking into.

O

When it's near the end of July, I have something more to write. No one's around when I retrieve the pale blue diary hidden in the back of my dresser drawer. As I pull it out, I find it unstrapped with the pewter lock wide open. My heart surges in anger and hissing snorts come from my nose. *Damn it. Jerk.* I fume, wondering which sister would dig through my dresser.

It wasn't Chase. She's only in first grade, so she can't read too much. It's Helen. She finally found it. I bet she picked the lock. I hope she didn't have time to read everything. She forgot to latch it. *How stupid.*

I want to kick something. There's nowhere to hide anything in this house. I've spent almost two months writing things down in the diary, including some secrets. Why would Helen want to look at my diary when she doesn't read much? Well, if it's because Helen thinks that I write about her—sometimes I do.

What a nosy little—I'm going to read everything one last time to decide whether my diary is going bye-bye.

MY DIARY

June 2: First Sunday—OH NO

Helen, Chase, and I went to church today for the first time—big deal. I am disappointed and I bet my sisters are too, but we aren't saying one word to each other about it.

A religious belief is a person's private business, maybe because nobody can see God. I just don't get it and it seems kind of crazy to me how adults fight over it. Since I've never heard of children fighting about religion, maybe I'll just stick to elementary school.

June 9: Second Sunday—OFFERING PLATE

When the minister said a prayer and everyone prayed, a wood offering plate was passed around. When it came to me, I put my money in and handed it to Helen.

Helen put her money in. Then her hand closed around a larger bill before she passed the plate to the man on her right.

When she did it, I made the sound of a big "oh" like a slurping-it-up "oh." Helen folded her hands like she was praying so she could hide the money in her lap. She pretended not to hear me, but I know she did because I was right next to her.

If the man sitting next to Helen heard me, he didn't turn to look. Maybe some people don't close their eyes to pray. What would they do if they saw her—stand up right in the middle of a prayer, point, and yell, "This little girl just stole some money from the offering plate!"

When I think about Helen taking that money, it's crazy enough to make me laugh. I'm shocked that she did it, but I find it hard to blame her when we both heard the minister talk about giving and receiving.

We don't bring it up. Thanks to Chase asking if Santa comes to Jesus's house, we talked about Santa instead. She's not mad at me anymore for not telling her he isn't real.

June 16: Third Sunday—CHURCH + BIBLE SCHOOL

Helen, Chase, and I haven't learned enough about religion. I've had enough. Our minister is a nice man, but his sermons are boring. I daydream to get away.

Today, things got worse because there's more to church than just Sunday sermons. There's also religious education for children called Bible school and we were signed up.

No one asked us if we wanted to go, and we aren't happy about it. The other children are going because they haven't learned enough either.

Will the Bible stories be like Greek and Roman mythology? The legends of ancient Greek gods, goddesses, strange creatures, heroes, and mortals are different from anything I've ever read so far. Their adventures and lessons are more exciting than the fiction-nonfiction I've heard at this church next door.

I bet we looked like a blond stair-step trio of sadness walking to Bible school. We followed signs and arrows taped to doors to find our way there.

Bible school is in the kitchen, where two long tables and chairs were set up for us. Most of the class sits and fidgets.

After the teachers checked everyone in, our silver-haired

minister started talking. This is what he said:

"Everything written in this book is true because it's the word of God." No.

"Women caused the downfall of the human race." I don't believe it. Besides, men are stronger.

"Babies are sinners." Is this why children have to go to church? Something's not right.

I forgot to hide my face and the minister noticed me right away. He asked if he'd said something that I didn't understand.

Oh, I understood what he was saying all right. I didn't care that everybody was looking at me. I let him know this can't be correct, saying, "Who says this about babies when they're born? They haven't done anything wrong yet."

This is nuts. Can he only read and agree? Well, I can read too, but I'll think for myself.

Helen and I just stared at each other. Chase's reaction surprised me the most. She shook her head and folded her arms like she was mad at the minister for calling babies sinners. Chase loves babies and animals and didn't even try to hide her sour face. I didn't know she had it in her.

I want to rebel and find a way to get kicked out of Bible school before it ends with confirming our faith and being confirmed.

Confirmation sounds like the Pledge of Allegiance we do in school. I'm still a little girl and I don't know what you're about yet—and besides, you have to earn my pledge. Is my hand going to have to go up higher? That's what I want to find out before giving my word of honor. That sounds about right and fair enough to me.

Yes, my mother's family came here for freedom of religion. Well, I'm all for freedom of religion too.

After Bible school, I asked Mother if there's really a God. She didn't take my question well. Then I asked if I could go to the synagogue. If it's not the right brand, at least I can learn another language. Well, that didn't turn out. Dad's not going to drive me and it's too far to walk.

June 18: Tuesday—THE ORGAN

To be fair, Helen isn't the only sister to misbehave in church. I have a few secrets.

Today, I sneaked into the church and ran up the aisle to the organ. I figured out how to make it play to the outside world. The music never blares during the week, and since it's not Sunday, I played only a few bars of what I made up—not church music—before shutting everything off. I ran out before anyone saw me. I bet my mother heard it, but she hasn't said anything about it.

June 19: Wednesday—THE LOVE CLUB

Before school let out for the summer, five of us started a club.

First, we worked out our plan. We would bolt out of our seats when the teacher switched off the lights and before she turned on the TV. We knew that no one could see much of anything until their eyes adjusted to the darkness. That would be the time to make a blind run for the coat closet in the back of the classroom.

While everyone else watched the screen, we had fun sitting close together on a long bench in the closet. We could talk in there. It wasn't easy to keep it quiet when someone's jokes were funny. We still listened since the dangerous part of our plan was getting back to our seats right as the TV lesson ended.

When the teacher walked from her desk to turn the lights back on, her back was to the class. This was when we rushed back to our seats. A few of us ran all the way from the second row and back, but we made it.

Just five of us belong to the Love Club. I will not write the real names of our members here in case somebody reads my diary because it's a secret club. We picked this name for our club because we kiss in the coat closet.

June 19: Wednesday—EXPLORING

Ty doesn't go to our church. Maybe he doesn't go at all. I never asked him. We like to explore buildings—especially old, abandoned ones—so today I invited him to wander around the church with me.

The church's heavy wood front door with its iron rod handle was unlocked. When we let ourselves in, the door closed behind us without any noise. We stood for a moment in the entryway.

I whispered for him to choose our direction and pick any door since he's never been there. Ty pointed to the double doors on the right. This part is called the nave—I looked it up. We both love music, so right away, we ran up the aisle past the minister's podium and straight for the organ. He fingered the keys and we agreed to come back to play it if we found the church empty.

We tiptoed to the balcony. It's a safe spot, so we sat down for a minute. Ty leaned over to kiss me on the cheek and reached for my hand. We didn't speak because we still didn't know if we were alone in the building or not. Ty and I held hands while looking down at the wood pews and long windows on either side of the aisles. The Bibles and hymnbooks were in their holders on the back of every pew. Nothing was upside down or out of place, so no one needed to come in and fix things.

When we walked back to the entryway, we almost got caught. Ty's hand was just about to touch the minister's office door when the minister and church elders started talking. Ty and I just looked at each other for a second.

In case they heard us, we raced to the older part of the church that I know is empty most of the week. We knew the men wouldn't come if we were quiet. If they did need to come to this part of the church, we'd hear them and have time to hide. We found our hiding spot under the stage stairs and talked and kissed. It was so much fun that we're coming back to explore and play games.

How Do I Know?

Our Thursday hiking plans got canceled because Bill is sick. So, Ty came over in the early afternoon. As soon as Ty parked his bike inside our screen porch, we left to start exploring the church.

After the close call yesterday, we decided to walk around the block to the older part of the church. We got in through a side entrance. No one is ever in here on weekdays. I know because it's my secret rainy-day reading place. Ty called this church an antique because it's painted white except for the floors, hardware, and the belfry shutters below the steeple.

Ty didn't see it yesterday, so we sneaked back to the reception room, where we have family-night potluck dinners every month. It's what I like about church—eating and playing games with the other children.

We ran back to the old white church nave. It looks like a theater without the pews. We climbed the stairs to the stage and danced together. I even did a few cartwheels.

Then we decided to relax under the stairs, where we had so much fun yesterday. We talked, giggled, and kissed until Ty said, "Strip for me."

Has Ty has lost his mind? Strip for me? Why? I'm just a little girl, so there's nothing to see.

"No," I said.

"Nameless did," Ty said, like this would change my mind.

"Well, that's <u>Nameless</u>," I replied. I don't care if <u>Nameless</u> did. I'm not.

What Ty asked doesn't make any sense to me. Until now, he did what I asked, and I did what he asked because we've each liked what we've asked, and we've always agreed with each other.

Ty and I were quiet when we walked back to my screened porch, and he rode away on his bike. He wasn't mad and I wasn't either.

"I didn't give him what he wanted, so that's the end of him." I don't even know why I said this to myself.

I won't forget. I will remember what happened forever.

June 21: Friday—SO THAT'S HOW IT IS

I still can't believe what Ty wanted me to do yesterday. I didn't tell anyone. Not Relia and not Chloe—nobody. Most of all, I didn't tell <u>Nameless</u> what I knew she'd done either.

The phone rang and I beat Mother to it. It was Ty and he wanted to see me right away. Not just that, but he wanted to go to our private place in the church to talk. "That sounds good," I said. It was all I could say because Mother was right there.

Ty and I were under the church stairs talking like nothing happened yesterday. Soon we were back at it—making plans, telling jokes, and holding hands. Ty asked me to close my eyes. I did, but I thought, "Uh-oh. I hope I haven't made a big mistake by coming here today."

Ty lifted my hand and asked me to keep my eyes closed. I felt something slide over my finger. "Now you can open them," he said while holding my hand up for me to see.

I've never been this surprised. On my left hand was a gold wedding band. It even fit perfectly.

Ty kissed my hand and then he kissed me on the lips. I felt so happy that he was still my friend, so I kissed him back. Ty never asked me to strip again.

So, that's how it is. I get a wedding ring because I didn't strip— hmm. Is this crazy or what? I don't understand it.

June 23: Fourth Sunday—FINALLY, THE END OF C + BS

Everyone was given a Bible today. Helen and Chase put their Bibles down on the table in front of them like the rest of the children, and that was it.

Since I'm the curious reader, I opened mine and looked through the book's chapters for female names to find out what they did. What did they do? That's weird. These women must not have powers and adventures like the Greek goddesses.

Male mortals like Jonah, Moses, Joseph, and Jesus had powers and adventures. The minister called them prophets and one was the son of a god. Their wild stories sound more like mythology than history.

Isn't Bible school supposed teach us how to do what these men did? Our minister is a religious scholar, but he never showed us how the prophets learned to use their talents to accomplish their feats. Maybe he didn't know. The bad news—we never did find out how.

The whole class was bored enough to throw Bibles to each other as though they were on fire. Our forgiving Sunday school teachers were more patient than our elementary school teachers.

The good news—we're through with Bible school. We can parrot prayers, stories, and laws. Somehow, we made it through without anyone getting kicked out.

June 30: Fifth Sunday—SERMON QUESTIONS

If the religious sermon is supposed to be the living word, why is it so dead around here? Where is the life?

I sometimes wonder the same thing about school because the action is happening outside the window, so then I answer myself. Life is outside.

July 7: Sixth Sunday—I AGREE

Nothing about the sermon was different except for today's message. Our minister preached like he believed what he said was true. Jesus walked on water and people saw him do it too. I squirmed, turning to give my sisters one of those looks. I was ready to ask a question when the minister announced the page number for the hymn and the organist began to play.

Everyone was saved by the church music. So was I. The congregation stood with their hymnbooks and started singing.

I did too, but my mind was blaring. We had science demonstrations in school to see what materials float or not.

Chase, Helen, and I looked at each other. We just shook our heads at the minister's words. Next came the prayer, so everyone sat down. Helen and Chase looked down. So did I, but without closing my eyes.

My mind rebelled. As my thoughts continued to broadcast, I felt the movement of someone returning to the pew and a man spoke directly to me, saying, "Don't believe everything you read in this book. Pick out the truth and put all of the books together."

I felt so relieved that I wanted to hug him. Yes. Finally. There's another sane person in the room. I wanted to talk to him and let him know that I agreed with him, but when I raised my head to thank him, no one was there.

He wasn't sitting by me, and everyone was seated. I looked around the entire room to find him. All eyes were on the minister at the pulpit. This message obviously hadn't come from any of them. No one was looking in my direction.

There's no way the man could have gotten away, but where was he? I had some questions for him.

Put all of the books together—which books are all of the books?

Then it dawned on me. He wasn't a regular person. He was a visitor spirit.

Helen and Chase would have told me if they heard the man. This lets me know they can't hear like me. I do wonder if these things are happening to anyone else.

Some things haven't changed since I was four years old. I heed the advice of my wise invisible visitors. This male spirit must be one of these good ones too.

His advice sounded correct, so I've decided to follow it and do just that—pick out the truth and put the books together. It reminds me of a task given to a mortal in Greek mythology. This is a huge job, and I know it will take time.

Well, I didn't expect anything this exciting to ever happen in church. The spirit's message is one that I'll have to keep to myself.

I've prudently realized I have two families, but they live in different worlds. The family I see every day doesn't know me at all—at least not this curious part of me.

Where is the real life? My answer is different this time.

Where is the real life? Part of it is inside me.

4

THE BLACK ANGEL DRESS

The front door opens. "Who smells like a French whore?" Chuckling follows.

Shea's mom is home from her job at a real estate office. The click-clacks of high heels move closer to Shea's bedroom, where she and I are talking.

"Mom's following her nose," says Shea, who isn't bothered by fragrances.

"Ha ha. I didn't know scents could travel so far. Oh. Here's Chanel No. 5. My mother only wears Chanel. I already know how it smells," I tell her.

Shea has samples of nearly every scent carried by the department store. She watches me dab and spray fragrances while I sit on the stool in front of her girlie vanity table set and mirror. My neck is full of test sites, and I've covered the entire surface of both arms with cologne and perfume until there's no room left for anything else.

Shea and I are still giggling about the word *whore* when her mother walks in. Lily is a pretty brunette, casual in her manner and nicely dressed. When she glances in the mirror to check the tidiness of her hair, which is done in a sophisticated French twist, she gives Shea a big hug and our eyes meet.

My face flushes as I say, "Guess who reeks?" Lily blows me a kiss from a safe distance and laughs some more.

Shea and I are both fourteen, and Lily knows we're just experimenting with beauty products. Shea is already wearing foundation and powder. Face makeup is too much of a mask for me. It never matches my skin anyway. Even Shea agrees that it looks odd on me.

Maybe I take after my mother. A few of her art-major college friends put makeup on her for a photo shoot. It ruined their class project. Mother is a natural beauty with perfect skin. Their photographs would have turned out well if they'd left her face alone. I bet she looked like something dead from a horror movie.

"Girls, I have some good news. I'm driving to the lake in Maryland on Saturday. Would you both like to go? My sister's family and a few friends will be there."

Shea is all in. "It'll be a lot of fun, Diana. Boys too," she whispers.

Lily coos as though remembering her own teenage years. "Boys close to your age will be there."

How Do I Know?

I catch Shea's eye and wink. Shea and her mom are fun to be around. Lily is funny and says what's on her mind. She doesn't judge us the way some adults might. It encourages and influences Shea and me to do the same. I want to stay young at heart like Lily when I grow older and never forget the early years of my life.

"It sounds like fun," I say. I've never been swimming in a lake— only in pools and the ocean. I have a brand-new swimsuit too. "I'll ask my parents and be right back."

Lily and Shea watch from the bedroom window as I run through their backyard. Shea and I visit each other so much that our footsteps heading back and forth have created a trail. I follow it through the vacant, weedy field between her backyard and mine.

On Saturday morning, Shea and I help her mom pack for the two-hour trip to the lake. Drinks and food for the picnic fill two coolers. Once the car is loaded, we head north.

I sit next to Shea and behind the front passenger seat. We talk and joke or sing to pass the time. The landscape starts with busy cities and towns. In the countryside, animals graze in the fields of ranches where scarcely a person is seen. Orchards, groves, and rows of crops on farmlands come into view. Many shades of green whiz past our windows.

About an hour into the drive, a new favorite song of mine starts playing. No one else sings along, so I listen to learn it. Then, the sound goes out just before the second chorus. This part is the most fun to sing and I don't want to miss it.

"What happened? The song just cut out. Could you please turn the music back on, Lily?"

I know she heard me, but the song doesn't resume and nothing else plays. There's only silence. Lily turns and stares very pointedly at me, as though she can't understand what I was asking.

"What?" I'm puzzled.

"Nothing was ever on." Lily's face has a strange look.

Nothing was ever on? I'm speechless. Where could the conversation go from here?

Everything is quiet until Lily and then Shea erupt into giggles. *Maybe they think I'm joking.* Their laughter gives me the kind of contagious giggles that, once started, won't stop. Lily's upper body rocks back against her seat and then shoots forward into the steering wheel. Her deep belly laughing causes her to bounce up and down. She clings to the steering wheel while her body bobs up, back, left, and right—sometimes moving like the letter *x* or around in a circle.

I think Lily might have to pull over. Her movements make Shea and me laugh even harder. Shea hugs her stomach, trying to catch her breath. She is crying laughing. Her mascaraed brown eyes squeeze out tears of glee. We are hysterical and experience a round-and-round chain reaction of shrieking laughs. Finally, our laughing jag slows to periodic titters.

We've inhaled and exhaled the laughter's air deeply. Its results produce a time of quiet.

How Do I Know?

My attention returns to the woodsy scenery and flickering sunlight patterns scattering on trees. A grove surrounded by a forest rushes by.

Questions come and go. More questions arise. *Did I have an antenna or two? How about another me upside down on top of my head? Seriously, how did I hear every detail of the song so perfectly if no device was on in the car?*

Lily said nothing was ever on. That hasn't solved anything to my mind. I keep my questions to myself, deciding that it's best to say nothing more. It will be easier left as a joke.

"We should be at the lake in about ten minutes, girls."

"Yay!" We respond from the back seat.

When we arrive, Shea and I pile out of the car. She hobbles and then shakes her legs like they've been asleep.

Lily gets out and stretches. "We've arrived at Deep Creek Lake. Isn't this a perfect-looking spot with its own beach? By the way, it has shallow water a long way out before it gets deep."

"It's beautiful," says Shea, and I nod in agreement. We wave to a small group of people coming to help us carry the coolers. Two boys are among them.

Relatives and family friends surround the car. A boy with dark brown hair introduces himself to me. Shea smiles and moves her head almost imperceptibly in a way that tells me it's fine to go ahead without her.

"Let's walk to the lake," the boy suggests.

"Okay," I say. We're knee deep in the water when I confess, "Robert, I can't really swim, but that won't stop me from jumping in."

"Don't worry, Diana. I can," he replies.

Everyone just watches from the shore. No one swims out to interrupt us. I think they realize how connected he and I are all at once. It's rare to be the only people in the lake. Robert and I come ashore just a few times the entire day.

O

It's funny how time revs like an engine when you're having fun and idles like an atomic clock stuck in neutral when you're not. The sun must have ejected some of its corona; the moon must have exerted some extra pull, increasing the rotation of the earth—kicking gravity out of the way to speed up time. The day was over. The sun was starting to set, and everyone was calling it quits—everyone but Robert and me.

I knew by the end of the day that I'd made a friend. All of us hugged as we said our goodbyes. No one even minded that Robert and I hadn't spent the day with the group.

"We'll have to do this again. Let's not wait so long," said Lily. Deep Creek Lake was one of her favorite places to see her loved ones.

"We'll be sure to bring Diana back with us." Shea looked directly at Robert and then me.

Robert gave me a wistful look. "I'll come visit you when I get my driver's license. Until then, I'll call you."

"Yes, we'll keep in touch. I'd like that," I said.

Lily honked three goodbyes and turned the headlights on before driving off. Shea and I waved until everyone was out of sight. We were barely away from the lake when Shea started talking about Robert.

"Robert is my favorite cousin. We've known each other since we were babies. People thought we were twins when they saw us."

"Yes, they did," said Lily. "Genetics and both of you having brown eyes and hair helped with that. Robert is my absolute favorite nephew. Now only the two of you know. Don't tell your aunt Sara."

"I always suspected that he was, Mom. I won't say a thing to Auntie. Diana, we've never seen Robert so serious."

"You two sure make a cute couple," said Lily.

"Mom."

"Do I sound like I'm in a hurry to make you part of our family?"

"Ha ha, Mom. We like your teasing."

"We do and I do," I said. Lily caught that and laughed at my joke. "I liked Robert right away. He's respectful, so I didn't feel like prey at all," I told them.

"Not like the jerky who lives next door to you." Shea knew all about him.

"Please enlighten me," requested Lily.

I poked Shea and whispered, "You tell her."

"As soon as Diana's parents leave, jerky calls her. He's always watching and waiting like a stalker for his chance to pounce."

"It's annoying," I said. "I don't dare tell my dad. He doesn't have much patience for males who don't respect females. He would like Robert, though."

"If you ever feel like you can't handle a situation, please tell me or another responsible adult. Both of you are pretty girls. Some males aren't mature or informed. They can lose their heads. You can always come talk to me if anyone makes you feel uncomfortable."

"Mom has strong feelings about the lack of education in our society."

"She's right. Maybe jerky just hasn't been trained yet," I said.

Lily added, "The apple sometimes doesn't fall far from the tree—you know that old expression. Unacceptable behaviors can be passed down through generations."

"You see why I can talk to Mom about everything?"

"Yes. That's how I feel about Robert," I said. "We talked like we had lots of catching up to do. I can't swim well, so when the water reached my neck, Robert carried me. He wasn't going to let me drown."

Shea whispered, "Did he kiss you? We had our eyes on you two, but we couldn't tell."

"Shh. We ducked under the water and kissed a few times. It's romantic because the light is beautiful there. Flowing hair looks like a mermaid's too." Loudly, I said to Lily, "Robert and I had a fantastic time at the lake."

"We thought so," said Lily, chuckling. "Robert is mature and keeps his word. He'll come visit you when he gets his license."

O

Life suddenly changes after my first year of high school. Shea and Lily move away. My parents buy a home in the boonies. It's being built and will be ready before school starts.

Something has remained steady. Robert calls me once a week and we have fun on the phone. Just like it was at the lake, we never run out of things to say.

Today, he has good news. "The band is rehearsing tonight, so I bought some new drumheads. We may get into songwriting for the first time too."

"That's exciting. Hum one for me next time we talk—even if it's not finished. You have a nice voice."

"I'll do that if we succeed." Robert laughs. "By the way, you like falling asleep listening to music like I do."

"It's been my favorite thing to do since elementary school. I just need to keep the sound low. I don't have any headphones yet."

"You will. Save up that babysitting money. I almost forgot—I just got my learner's permit."

Before I can congratulate him, the kitchen suddenly disappears as the view shifts to inside my mind. A shining object breaks through the darkness. It's a car.

"Oh. I . . . Robert? I'm not sure what this is, but I need to tell you because it's odd. My mind was dark until I saw a flash of white light. I don't know why, but I see a yellow and white station wagon and that's it. It's just hanging in the air and moving—yet it's not moving away. It's like a clear photo, but everything else around it is dark. This has never happened, and I don't know what it means. I don't know anyone with a car like that, do you?"

"It's not familiar to me either. Maybe we're going to write a car song tonight. I'd like to talk some more, but I need to pick something up at the grocery store for Mom for dinner."

"Congratulations on getting your learner's permit. I'm going for a walk around the neighborhood. There's going to be a basement dance party this weekend. I'm helping with the decorations today."

"Have fun. I'll call you next week," says Robert.

"Good luck with your songwriting. Bye."

After we hang up, I walk around our neighborhood of brick homes, mature trees, and hedges. I check in on the boy who is throwing the dance party. Soon, other teenagers show up to help. Our theme is cards. Using markers, we draw large playing cards on poster paper and decorate these with glitter and streamers before attaching them to the walls. We string lights, add folding chairs, and rearrange some furniture to make more space for a dance floor with a booth area for the DJ. After that, I walk home.

The phone rings just as I open the back door. Mother answers it and calls out, "It's Robert."

"Robert? Twice in one day? Thanks, Mother."

"Diana?" His voice is different.

"Hi, Robert. What's going on? Everything okay?"

"I couldn't wait until next week to call you. You saved me from a terrible accident. I'm still trying to calm down from it."

"What happened?"

"It's about that car you saw. If you hadn't told me, I would have been in a bad accident. I was driving to the store and saw a yellow and white station wagon in my rearview mirror—just like you described. The light turned red, but it wasn't stopping. I pulled off the road right before it slammed into the car waiting at the light. Both cars were totaled. The driver was pried out of that station wagon. Ambulances came and took both drivers to the hospital. I owe you my life today and I can't thank you enough."

"Oh." I'm shaking. "Our friendship means a lot—maybe that's why I saw the car. I wanted to be an angel, but there's no diploma for that job," I say, letting out my secret.

"Ha ha. Well, you got your wings today."

O

Our new house is ready. We've just moved to a new neighborhood and I'll be going to a new high school. Orientation is in a week. It doesn't take long to make new friends. Twelve of us are new in this new neighborhood, and we take a forty-five-minute bus ride to a new school. Forty-five minutes from nowhere to somewhere.

School is boring and repetitive. Socializing could be a class. Should be a class. Well, maybe I've found the ultimate in socializing by selecting a new elective: art.

Today is the first day of art class. The classroom is extra large with a wall full of windows, and there are tables and chairs instead of desks. Art supplies—paints, clay, brushes, pens, inks, papers, tools, canvases, wood, fabric, metal plates, and chemicals—have been placed atop long shelves above the counters lining three sides of the room. Finished samples using these art materials are on display.

Laughter comes from behind me. Turning around, I note a girl casually slouched in a chair. Next to her is a boy wearing a T-shirt and jeans. They're sharing a magazine like a couple, or maybe they're friends. She has just pulled it away to read something, and they have another laugh.

I walk to the back of the room, put my notebook and purse on the table in front of them, then ask, "Is it all right if I sit here?" The magazine is now flat, and it looks like the cover is hiding a homemade book on the inside.

"Sure." The boy nods, making no attempt to hide the book.

"Fine with me," says the girl, straightening up a little bit in her chair.

Moments later they're back to it. Their banter is amusing, so I turn around with an approving look and a grin.

They notice, and we introduce ourselves. That's how I meet Jamie and David. My first impression is that both are smart, sweet, and irreverent.

A few classes later, I sit next to them. David shares his cartoons with Jamie and me. He can draw as quickly as I scribble notes in history class.

Jamie, David, and I have the same humor, and we don't need to steal conversations because a lot of talking goes on while creating. It's even allowed by our art teacher, Mr. D, until we get his stink-eye signal for being too loud. There's freedom to express yourself in this classroom. We're serious students, but we have fun.

"Diana, would you like to see the sculpture I'm working on—when you have a minute?" David watches as I work.

My project is a piece of wood about thirty-six inches long that stands vertically like an obelisk. I'm painting intricate designs and codes on it with black ink. "Good timing. The ink on this part needs to dry. Ready," I tell him after cleaning my pen. "Where's your sculpture?"

"On the front table," he says, motioning for me to walk ahead of him. David points to a clay bust of a male about twenty inches tall with an alert gaze, layered shoulder-length hair, and a face that belongs in a romance novel.

"It's the best one here. When did you do it?"

"Mr. D let me work on it after class. It took a few hours."

"He's beautiful. Is it you?" As soon as I say it, my face starts burning, so I look back at our table.

David fiddles with his piece, turning it around to critique it. "The clay isn't dry yet, so I can still make changes if I spray it with water and cover it with plastic. It's a musician—one of the best guitarists around today."

"So, you like music?"

"Yeah. I listen to everything. It's my education for writing."

"Your songs? Are you taking music lessons? Are you in the school band?"

David looks amused by my questions. "Yes. I write my own songs. No lessons yet because I can play by ear. I'm not with the marching band." He demonstrates a crazy elastic march with some exaggerated neck action.

Surprised, I can't hold back and shriek with laughter. Mr. D glares at me and I flush—right to my cheeks.

David rolls his eyes and shakes his head. "Let's get you back to that piece you're working on. It's good. I've never seen anything like it," he whispers as we return to our table.

"Thanks. There's a secret language hiding in the patterns. I have maybe two hours of work before it's finished."

How Do I Know?

He and I watch Jamie dig into a linoleum block with a V-shaped chisel to scoop out an image of a dog. A silly photo she's using as a reference is propped up against a book.

"Is this really your dog? Why haven't I ever seen him?"

Jamie keeps carving into her linoleum plate as she explains, "He's our new puppy. My little sister takes him for afternoon walks—that's why. He's a bichon with a head like a cotton ball and his name is Argot. He's always sticking his tongue out. It's funny, but I thought glasses would make him look even more ridiculous. I took this photo before he shook off the glasses and snorted like he was talking."

David has been sketching and already has a cartoon of Jamie at work with her long hair piled up on her head and held in place by two thin paintbrushes. Argot's image looms large in the foreground. It's only missing the right caption. We laugh when David asks, "Is Argot the short version of escargot?"

I'm silent for the most part when working on my piece. Painting with a tiny brush or ink pen is a slow process, and it's too near the end of class to do much more. "Mr. Cock-A-Doodle-D is going to chime any minute," I say, cleaning my tools.

David walks with me to my next class. This leads to meeting each other between classes and passing notes and even snacks back and forth in the hall. His writing style is honest, amusing, and laugh-out-loud funny, and he always includes drawings and cartoons. I can't draw as well as he does, but I draw the best I can—mainly faces and designs with some fancy lettered captions in the margins. I've never written this many notes or eaten so many sunflower seeds in their shells—all in one day.

O

Getting on the bus for the forty-five-minute trip home makes me wish that I lived closer to Jamie and David. They've known each other since elementary school and live on the same street a few miles away from the high school. My neighborhood is the farthest away.

"Kay." I wave and call out to my best friend, who is already on the bus. She's a leggy brunette with thick hair that reaches her waist. Her house is close to mine. Kay sits next to Deb, our other best friend, who lives just around the corner.

"Alina loaned me the book. I have it here," Deb whispers excitedly. She's sophisticated beyond her years—very graceful, quiet, and genuine. Kay and I excel at getting Deb out of her melancholy moods.

"How are we going to see it together?" Kay is never one to leave anyone out.

"The back seat. Hurry. I'll grab us a spot." Riding in the back is an uneven adventure that causes much bumping up and down plus a few actual moments of being airborne—almost like a free carnival ride. "There's more privacy back here for the subject." I want to yell this to the whole bus, but I just say it under my breath. I pick a window seat and Kay sits down with Deb in the middle.

Just like us, Deb's old friends live too far away to see often. But Alina stayed at Deb's last weekend. Kay and I were invited to meet Alina, who had a pierced nose, a circle necklace with a star in it, and many rings with insignias. She wore black and deep purple and didn't hide the fact that she thought of herself as a witch.

"Alina thinks I have two good best friends now. She remembered that you wanted to see this book," says Deb.

"Maybe it'll tell us what witches do," I whisper. The witch label makes me feel uneasy, but I don't know exactly why.

"Could a green thumb with plants be a witch's spell?" Practical Kay would come up with that question.

"That's a plant-loving person or some good farming. I talk to my plant and named it Abby Normal. It's growing all over my bedroom," I say. Deb and Kay laugh.

"Good witch," Deb teases. "Let's pick some spells." She whispers their titles until Kay stops her.

"A spell to become invisible." Kay sounds dubious.

"This I have to see," I say. *Right. If this were true, people would be appearing and disappearing all over the place.*

"Me too—I have to see because I'm an atheist." Kay thinks religion is completely made up.

"You won't believe this one then." Even pale Deb isn't that gullible. "I'll read it," she says. "A human skull, five bean seeds. On the night of a full moon, plant a seed in each eye, two seeds in the nose, and one seed in the mouth. Water and grow. When the plants are mature, take a bean from each orifice. Allow them to dry. Once dry, wait for the next full moon. Take these five beans and go outside just before midnight. Stand or sit in your sacred spot. Hold the beans in your mouth to be invisible."

Kay and I shake our heads. She twists her long brown hair with a few fingers to get it out of the way, saying, "What does the illustration look like? A blank page?" She and I grin as we lean over for a closer look.

Deb ignores us and flips the page. It shows a skull with a bean in each orifice. "Where can we get a human skull?" she wonders aloud.

"Why, do you want to try it? It's fun to imagine it working, but there's no way this spell is real." I look straight into Deb's clear pool-blue eyes, which often appear too tragic for someone our age.

Deb pinches her lower lip with her thumb and first finger before answering. "I don't believe this one would ever work, but I noticed a spell called "sacred space." Do you mind if we go back to it? It might have something to do with this spell." Deb is not giving up on spells yet.

"Is sacred space different from sacred spot?" I just throw the question out there. Maybe Deb knows.

"Uh. Maybe it's a dot or a circle," says Kay.

"Or a G-spot. Okay, let's hear it," I say.

Kay and I almost have a laugh attack. A sacred space doesn't sound beyond belief, but we need a witch dictionary.

"This explains it," says Deb. She lightly smooths the page with her fingertips before reading in a low voice. "Choose a place—indoors or outdoors. Define the shape of this space and decorate it any way you wish. Natural materials like a circle of stones, leaves, branches, or flowers can mark it. When you go to your sacred space, create it as a positive, light, loving, relaxing, and safe space."

"Get ready for it." Deb smiles. The illustrations draw us into a three-headed huddle.

"That's a witch? Look—she's a good one." Kay sounds surprised. "So, my study area could be a sacred space too." Kay turns it into a matter-of-fact possibility.

"That would work. Put what makes you feel positive there," Deb says, closing the book. "Have a look if you want to see more spells." Kay shakes her head. I accept Deb's offer because I want to see the illustrations.

Deb and Kay talk about their issues at home while I look at the book. Then Kay recalls a witch story she'd forgotten about.

"My grandfather had allergies. He couldn't get any relief because nothing worked. Somebody told him about a witch doctor."

"What's that?" Deb asks.

"He said it was a woman who lived in the woods and helped people with her homemade remedies."

"She sounds like a witch, but not a doctor. Why did she live in the woods?" Deb is curious.

"Uh. To be closer to the plants she grew? I'm not sure. Anyway, when he described his symptoms, the witch doctor knew what to do. She picked plants from her garden and dried herbs from her kitchen, then crushed them in a bowl. She added her own liquids, then stirred and strained her brew. Then, she handed my grandfather a cupful, telling him to drink all of it, and he did. After that, he never had allergies again."

"Wow. So a witch doctor makes her own medicines. Nice story," says Deb.

Finally, the bus is on the long country road heading to nothing but our homes. It's a drive with curves, overhanging tree branches, and green tangles of low growth.

"Just in time." I hand the book back to Deb. "Thanks. I found out more about spells."

Deb is beaming. "It would be boring here without both of you."

"Boyfriends may come and go, but friends are forever," jokes Kay, making us laugh.

"You're my favorite best friends," I say, thankful to live close by.

We get off the bus at our stop. Tomorrow, we'll meet back here to catch up on anything new or unresolved.

O

My family's house is one of the prettiest on the street, landscaped with boxwoods, dogwood trees, and flowers. I let myself in and hear my parents talking about dinner.

"Hi, Diana. It's for you." Mother's voice comes from the kitchen. *She must have the hearing of a bat because I didn't make a sound.*

"Hi, honey," booms Dad.

"Hi and hi. Back at you." I drop my purse and pack at the bottom of the stairs. There's a package from Robert on the bench in the foyer. Inside, above the tissue paper, is a small envelope with my name on it. I open it first.

Hi Diana,

Thank you for those eyes of yours. I've been searching all over for months to find just the right present. It's for saving my life and protecting me from a terrible accident. I can't thank you enough.

Your long-distance friend,

Robert

Inside the tissue paper is a beautiful dress with a label that reads Black Angel Dress. Right away, I grab my things and run upstairs to try it on before dinner.

I view the dress in front of the full-length mirror in my parents' bedroom. It's black and short with an empire waist and long flared sleeves. I raise both arms, creating wings to look like a black angel. Wearing my new dress makes me feel like a celestial being. It even fits.

No one in school has anything like it. I decide to wear it tomorrow. I know it may look like a witch dress, but I don't care. I'll set that right.

Maybe I do have a witch story—one I've never told anyone. It's creepy and I don't know what it means.

It started when I was in elementary school—for no reason. It didn't fit my reality. I was enjoying myself to the max, having the time of my life pursuing all kinds of activities. I adored my classmates, and I even had a boyfriend. School was easy and I was in the third grade.

One day as I sat in class giving secret glances to my friends while listening to our teacher, I heard something. It wasn't something that could be heard from the outside, but if it had been, everyone would have run out of the room in fear.

What I heard was a stranger's voice. It broke in like a bad criminal who hated me more than anything else in the world, and it said, "What's the matter—*cat* got your tongue?" The man hissed as he spoke and emphasized the word *cat*—spitting out the word like he hated them too.

None of the men I knew ever talked to anyone with a voice like that. I'd never heard his kind of tone in the horror movies I loved to watch to try to make myself scared. The truth is there was no logical reason for him to enter my mind. I'd never had a thought like that.

When compared to my life, he sounded nutjob crazy. The man

was consumed with hatred. He was a creep who sounded like he loved to kill. Maybe he loved to kill young girls. He must have thought I was someone else.

As a little girl, I was too sunny to dwell on it. I let it go, remembering it rarely because it didn't fit with my world at all. This unnatural intrusion remained an unsolved mystery.

The next day, I take off my coat when I get to school. The black angel dress must look like a Halloween costume because everyone I pass in the hall stares at it. I get stopped by students who want to get a better look or ask me about it.

Right before lunch, I rendezvous in the bathroom with Deb and Kay. When I duck inside, they are already there.

Deb spots me immediately. "Wow. Your dress is stunning. I love it. It's a witch dress." It would be to Deb.

"Where did you get that? You look fantastic." Kay doesn't see it as a witch dress.

"It's from Robert. I've only seen him once, but we've been friends ever since. We talk on the phone every week."

"Do you plan on being more than friends?" Kay asks. "Okay, I'll just say it. Do you like him more than your cartoon friend?" This is code for David.

"I don't know," I say. Kay is prying.

Deb moves closer to whisper, "What made him send that dress

like a gift from a genie?" Of course, Deb would ask the odd question or think of something mysterious. That's what I like about her.

Girls walk in and out of the bathroom. It isn't uncommon to stop and talk, just hang out, or even smoke covertly in here.

A visual check is needed, so I bend over to see how many pairs of legs are still in the bathroom stalls—just a couple. "There's a reason and it's weird. You promise not to tell?" I'm whispering and almost sounding like Deb now. I wait until both Kay and Deb agree. "I protected him from a bad car wreck and maybe saved his life." Lifting a finger to my mouth, I point to the stalls.

Kay whispers, "You've only seen him once. How'd you do that if you weren't there?" She has to understand my explanation.

"It's hard to explain," I say. "I saw a car in my mind while we were talking, and I described it. When he saw that same car while he was driving, he reacted. If he hadn't moved out of the way first, it would have slammed into him."

"Why did you see that car?" Kay isn't through yet.

"That's a tough question." Deb squeezes my arm gently.

"I wish I knew. It was like seeing the answer on a Magic 8 Ball without touching it, but instead of words, that car floated to the top on its own," I say.

"Congratulations. You are a witch." Deb acts like I just passed a test.

How Do I Know?

Witch. Witch eye. Funny, Robert didn't use that word. He used the word angel. Angel—that's the best choice to me.

"Well, maybe I'm an angel, but I'm late. I hope David's still waiting."

"Where?" Kay brings things down to earth. I'm relieved when she doesn't echo Deb's witch label.

"The cafeteria," I say, waving as I dash off.

O

It was a week after I revealed why I had received the black angel dress. I'd just walked out of history class and was heading down the hall to meet David when I was surrounded by a group of girls—like being cornered by five strangers without having any idea why. These weren't rude girls. So far, I hadn't encountered any hateful or unfriendly girls.

I looked at the bright side—even finding humor in my situation. *Would I be the blond interpreter among five brunettes?* Silly thought.

This wasn't a random event, though. It had been planned. The girls smiled. I smiled back, tilting my head to one side and then the other as I acknowledged each girl in a friendly way, which broke the ice for them.

The most petite and plucky girl shifted position, taking a step forward. "I'm dying to know—how'd you do it?"

Was she in the bathroom? Maybe she overheard Kay, Deb, and me whispering in there. I knew Deb would never gossip about what I said. Neither would Kay. I was sure of that. The angel dress itself could have helped spark an absurd buzz. *Well, I'm in luck. This isn't the sixteenth century, when being labeled a witch meant a death sentence.*

Since there was no way to answer her question, I just shot her a puzzled look.

That must have given courage to the next girl, who looked like her taller sister. "Are you a witch?" she asked. "Did you use witchcraft to get him?"

What? Use witchcraft? You must be kidding. "No," I said, smiling in amusement. "I'm not a witch."

A cute girl with a ponytail and a shy but eager voice asked, "Then, how did you do it?"

"We'd sure like to know," added the tallest girl politely.

Each girl looked at me expectantly. There was a brief silence. Finally, the girl wearing round black-rimmed glasses got to the point of the encounter. "How did you do it? We want to know how you got him. What is your secret? That's what we want to know. We've been trying to get him since the fifth grade." This was the most revealing piece of information.

Get him? Good question. I hadn't even thought about that.

They were talking about David. They'd gone to the same elementary school and junior high school as him, but I hadn't. Now, it was clear. They were asking for my help. I noticed they were looking up to me. It made me feel a burden of responsibility to give them solid answers.

"First of all, it wasn't witchcraft. I didn't put a spell on him. The truth is that David trusts me because I'm his friend. We're both creative, plus our sense of humor is similar. I think we have a relationship because we're friends first. Friendship is the big secret."

"Will you help us?" When the plucky girl asked, the rest of the girls bobbed in agreement.

"I'm not a witch and I can't make any promises, but I will try to help you. Okay, let's do it like this," I said, opening my notebook to a blank page and handing it to the first girl along with a pen. "I'd like each of you to write your name and the name of the boy you're interested in right next to it."

When all five girls had done that, I explained, "I'll create wishes for you. Meet me back here at the same time on Monday. I'll have a small bag for each of you to put under your pillow to sleep with so your dreams will help you too."

The girls thanked me and waved goodbye. I flew down the hall to catch up with David, who was already walking to his next class. "Delayed. I was having an unexpected heart-to-heart talk with the girls," I said.

The girls were way down the hall by now. I wasn't going to reveal their crushes. David probably already knew since he'd known them since elementary school.

"I thought that was your head in the middle of some students. One more class to go." David and I stopped at his locker. "Won't need

79

these books—PE."

"What are you doing this weekend, David?"

"I'm practicing bass and working on a song. How about you?"

"I'm picnic hiking with Kay and Deb and taking some crazy photos, then babysitting on Saturday. Just doing the usual and the unusual. That's about it so far."

"Ha. The unusual—I'll try to draw that one. By the way, what is picnic hiking?"

"Grazing while you walk." When David laughed at that, I added, "I hope you write an unusually unusual song."

"Hey, girl. See you on Monday. Zeebucknee." He sneezed.

"Bless you. Whoa, I mean stay well," I tease him.

I forgot. David's an atheist like Kay. There are some places where it's a bad thing to offer a blessing when someone sneezes because the devil might stay inside. Go figure.

O

A late night of babysitting gave me a fit of Sunday-morning yawns. Did I dare peek out the window and meet the sun's daggers? It was early and spells were on my mind. I tiptoed back upstairs with a steaming cup of coffee in hand and grabbed the notebook. With a dose of caffeine, my mind started moving.

Wiggling the pen over a blank page was like dousing for water, and that's how it began itself. My formula wasn't from Alina's book of spells—I made it up because a spell seemed like an art project with a recipe. My approach wasn't witchcraft. It was creativity. I wasn't a professional witch or even an amateur.

LOVE RECIPE

Five paper hearts

Ten sunflower seeds

Ten teaspoons of garden soil

Five birthday candles

Five matches

Five little bags

Five ribbons

First, I had to make sure my parents were occupied with a movie or something because my sacred space was the patio and picnic table. If they'd seen me, they would have wondered what was going on.

I was winging it, but I was serious and even wore the black angel dress. I carefully laid everything out on a large platter, adding scissors, a pen, a spoon, a feather, and an ashtray to the mix.

A. Wolfe

I started by cutting two names from the page in my notebook and placing these over a paper heart. As I held these pieces of paper, I lit a candle with a match, made silent wishes for the girl and boy, and said their names. I transferred the flaming paper to the ashtray, where it burned completely. To this little pile of ash, I added two teaspoons of garden soil, two sunflower seeds, and the candle and match. I stirred this mix before putting it into a small bag with the help of the feather. Then I tied the bag shut with the ribbon.

This was repeated four more times until there were five tidy little bags of spells to deliver the next day. I didn't have to explain anything to my parents.

On Monday, when the five girls surrounded me again, I had a bag to give to each one. They promised to get back to me about what happened. "The power of friendship works the best," I reminded them. They nodded and waved, and we scattered.

When Robert called, I let him know that the angel dress was my favorite outfit and popular too. No one could find a dress like it anywhere. All five of my best girlfriends had asked to borrow it. But before hanging up, I had to give him the news. The angel dress was passed around until my best friend's narrow-minded dad found it in her closet and beat her severely for wearing it. He burned the dress like a spell of his own while yelling and muttering and calling it evil. This is the part I didn't tell Robert. Her dad's actions reminded me of the lunatic voice I'd heard in elementary school.

The girls kept their promises and found me in the hall. The results were good. Three out of five girls were in relationships with the boy of their choice. The spell gave them something positive, but it couldn't take credit for their success like their confidence could.

How superstitious is the world now that we have science? It can't explain everything about reality. What is a witch? What does this single label even mean?

Seeing ahead in another dimension of time isn't a habit of mine. It isn't exactly witchcraft or religion. What is it then?

Physics.

5

SHE WHO IS TESTED

The well-dressed man standing at the foot of Lisa's bed motioned for her to follow him. She did. She got up. When her nose touched the bedroom wall, she found herself saying, "Wall? So what. No problem." Lisa drifted right through it in pursuit of the man.

Whenever the stranger came, he always appeared respectfully at the end of her bed. Feeling unalarmed by his late-night visits, Lisa followed him without hesitation. Leaving her bed and her home, she floated along with him to the outside world.

This was one of the more bizarre tales I would hear from an otherwise down-to-earth older coworker. She'd been described as reliable, careful, methodical, responsible, beautiful, honest, and a loving mother. I'd found this portrait of her to be true. By the time she told me about the man, I'd known her for close to three years, and I could tell you one thing—Lisa was not a crazy woman.

How Do I Know?

I first met Lisa when I was hired by her boss—a doctor. She was his office manager. Still a college student, I was hired as the office nurse. The job was perfect because it provided two-hour lunch breaks each day. This gave me time to study, take a two-hour nap on the x-ray table if I'd been out dancing the night before, or have lunch with Lisa in the office. I had plenty of time to do what I wanted, and that's how I'd gotten to know Lisa and her son, Alex, who phoned his mom every day. I talked to him whenever the front office got busy.

When Lisa invited me to her home, she insisted that I stay for the entire weekend. She said I would be good company for her Alex, who liked me because we enjoyed exploring weird phenomena.

She was excited for me to meet their newest family member—a pet parrot. The young yellow-naped Amazon was supposed to be a big talker, but Lisa couldn't get him to speak a single word. She hoped her bird would imitate me.

When it was the end of our workweek, Lisa and I left the doctor's office right at five o'clock. Alex was already home from school and waiting for us.

True to her nature, Lisa was a methodical driver. I doubted she ever drove over the speed limit, but the highway was too thick with cars to know for sure. Thirty minutes later, Lisa smoothly entered her driveway.

It occurred to me that maybe Lisa thought of me as a daughter and a sister to Alex. He and I got along like siblings, and Lisa was in the role of an old-fashioned mother. It was important to her that Alex and I keep our grades up. She cooked so we students could get our studying done. Her dinner of rotisserie chicken, roasted vegetables, potato pancakes, and Black Forest cake was delicious. Afterward, we had fun playing card games until midnight. That summed up Friday.

O

The following morning, Lisa opened the curtains to let in the sun as she gave me a tour of her large split-level home. Six feet tall, she easily plucked a yellowed leaf from a high hanging plant in the kitchen without a ladder. No detail escaped her attention.

There was no clutter or disarray. The rooms were decorated with a combination of Scandinavian furniture and inherited antiques.

Lisa and Alex lived in an established neighborhood where people liked to walk. That's what the three of us did—walked, talked, and munched Alex's trail mix blend.

Later in the evening, the five of us—including poodle and parrot—settled in the downstairs family room to watch a late-night comedy show. Lisa and Alex fell asleep halfway through it.

The parrot's cage was covered with a baby blanket. Not a peep came from the bird. Rosie, the café au lait miniature poodle, was asleep in her comfortable luxury dog bed.

Rosie didn't even flinch when I got up. I looked at the slumbering little family scattered around the room and decided not to wake them. I left the TV on.

The guest room was down the hall at the opposite end of the house. There was no guessing its location among the many closed doors along the way. It was the only room in the entire home without a colorful hand-painted Pennsylvania Dutch hex sign centered above the doorframe.

I entered the guest room and locked the door before admiring its beauty. Paintings of city scenes were grouped together on the wall above an antique chest. Placed on either side of a small table in front of the window were two fabric-covered chairs. A pale smoky-blue duvet cover on the bed matched the ceiling-to-floor linen drapes. The soft color gave the room a peaceful atmosphere.

My weekend bag was on a luggage stand in the closet. I put on pajamas after finishing my nightly routine. Still not ready to sleep, I felt around inside the bag for my textbook and closed the louvered closet doors.

When an hour had passed, I put the book away. Although I wasn't drowsy, I forced myself to turn off the light to get some sleep. Soon, I dozed off.

From a disturbance somewhere, but not in my dreams, came a single knock. Its powerful vibration penetrated my sleep.

Still not fully awake, I was dimly aware of being on my back. As I became a bit more conscious, I found myself on the right side of the full-sized guest bed with the queasy-foggy sensation of needing more sleep. *It's the dog.* Dangling my right arm in a listless pattern, I felt around for Rosie's curly little head.

Slow, measured sounds approached. Knock. Growl. Chains. The growl was *not* coming from Lisa's eighteen-pound dog. This realization jolted me wide awake.

There were a few seconds of quiet before the noises returned—closer now.

A single knock hit like a gigantic tree rammed against an immense gate. Its echoing boom was unearthly.

The growl followed. Terrible, long, and low—coming from a mouth with flesh-ripping teeth.

Chains rattled back and forth like a clapper swinging wildly inside a huge metal bell. The sound vibrated quickly. The heavy links sounded strong enough to contain a ferocious monster.

In the pitch-dark room, these awful repetitions continued until something landed on the bed. My stomach churned with the sudden trapping weight of a man, lion, or monkey pressing down on top of me.

I bit my lower lip to focus on the hurt. Breathing into the pain, I didn't move.

The midnight prowler didn't speak. When it roared, the sound was just above my ears. The full length of this intruder with its weight still on me was unbearable.

If you're evil—get out of here—go away. I focused my will like never before. Silently repeating this like a mantra caused my spine to line up as the words traveled deep into my core.

Finally, it moved. I don't know why it didn't harm or kill me. In a delayed reaction, my body began shaking uncontrollably. As soon as my legs could support me, I headed for the door.

In the pitch black, my hands touched the wall until I found the door, then the light switch. *Let there be some light.* I checked the door—still locked.

The bedroom looked unchanged. I took a few back-and-forth swipes at the drapes before opening them. Both windows were locked with the windowpanes intact. I searched the closet. There was no trapdoor to a crawl space on the floor and no such entry into the attic. Kneeling on my hands and knees, I had a look under the bed, finding nothing to obstruct my view—not even a few dust bunnies.

How did it get in? I was stumped and rattled, but I was sure it was gone—for now.

I don't believe in possession. It hadn't gotten under my skin. It hadn't possessed me—*good luck with that.* The creature landed on me, but it hadn't tried to rape me, unlike in the Jewish tales of incubi and succubae.

Was it the unnatural pet of Lisa's male visitor? Had this been its home?

The room's peaceful beauty allowed me to calm down enough to review my situation. If it came back, I'd get rid of it again. After smoothing the bedding, I fell back to sleep until morning.

O

My eyes didn't open gradually—they popped wide open. *Daylight. The door.* I checked like a person obsessed—it was still locked. Lisa and

Alex needed to be told because something broke into their house and what if it came back again?

After getting dressed, I headed upstairs. The wonderful aroma of coffee wafted a good morning. An artful table setting was in place in the dining room. Green cymbidium orchids and various fern fronds stood in a clear bowl vase in the middle of the table. Plates with bread, fruit, cheese, and meat had been placed on either side of the flower arrangement. Scattered around were small bowls of condiments. There was a big pot of coffee, milk, cream, and a pitcher of water positioned at one the end of the table.

I knew my news should not intrude upon the sunny atmosphere of this room. I decided to just wait. *Don't ask me how I slept, Lisa. You don't want to know.*

Both mother and son were already in the kitchen talking about eggs when I walked in. We said our good mornings, and Rosie got up from her pillow bed under the built-in desk to greet me. She wanted some attention, so I ran my fingers over her thick, curly hair. *You're sweet and spoiled. No way was that you last night unless you can turn into a lion.* I wanted to help, but Lisa made it clear that I was their guest and didn't need to do anything.

Alex and I headed to the dining room and waited for Lisa, who brought three poached eggcups to the table and said, "Eat them while they're hot." After she sat down, we whacked at our eggs with a knife. While cracking into mine, I hummed for their lonely pet bird downstairs in the entertainment room.

"We'll try that and see if our bird can carry a tune," Alex said.

"Babies mumble before they can talk."

"Let's be consistent, take it a step at a time and see what happens," Lisa advised her son. "Our bird needs to get to know us. Humming to it may be a good start."

After brunch, Lisa went downstairs to feed the young parrot. Alex and I were right behind her with Rosie following along. Their bird sat on its perch in captivity. The large cage had a swing but no chains. Lisa spoke to it like it was a baby, but the bird only looked at her. After eating seeds and a few grapes from bowls attached to the inside of the cage, the parrot was coaxed onto her finger.

Since we were all downstairs, it was my chance to talk about last night. "Thanks for inviting me to your home this weekend," I said.

"It's been my pleasure. I don't know why I didn't have you over sooner." The bird let Lisa massage its head. Maybe the grape had worked its magic.

"We're having fun with you here," said Alex as he closed his book. "You like what I like—weird things and comedy." His finger was still in *The Encyclopedia of the Paranormal* to mark where he left off. "This book is cool," he added. Without a doubt, he'd end up reading all of it right away.

"It looks good," I agreed. "I like reading what science figures out. But knowing what to believe isn't easy."

"You're right," said Alex, leaning down to pet Rosie, who'd jumped on his leg.

I turned to Lisa. "Your guest room is gorgeous. I love that pale shade of blue."

Lisa's eyes sparkled in response to my compliment. She cleared her throat before speaking. "It was a stretch for me to select everything and put the entire room together myself. You're our first guest since its renovation."

While wishing I didn't have to say anything, I couldn't let it go. *Wouldn't she want to know?* "Well, I need to tell you about last night. Something woke me up. At first, I thought it was Rosie, but the door was locked, so she couldn't have come in."

Alex moved his finger from the book, losing his place. I'd gotten his full attention.

In the calmest voice I could muster, I said, "I'm just going to say what happened." Being the messenger wasn't easy.

Poor Alex looked scared when I was finished. "What do you think it was?" He asked, gripping his book.

Lisa didn't wait for an answer. "Let's take a look. There must be a logical explanation."

We searched a bedroom, the home office, a bathroom, and the laundry room. Everything was immaculate and in perfect order, so the doors were pulled shut again.

Lisa opened the guest room door and went in first. Alex and I followed. After a search, nothing unusual was uncovered.

"Well, it must be the air conditioner," said Lisa.

"It can make a loud noise when it's first turned on, but it wasn't the air conditioner," I said firmly. *It was not the air conditioner.*

Lisa turned on the air conditioner. The motor made a clap and a hum. There was a brief swoosh of air from pressure in the ducts, then it quieted until there was not much sound at all.

"It seems okay, but I'll have it checked just to be sure," said Lisa.

"When did you hear the growl?" Alex asked.

"Around three—why?"

"That's when Rosie woke me up. She was howling at the top of her lungs," he said.

"Rosie howled?" Lisa asked with a worried look. "If you're afraid to sleep here one more night, there's another bedroom upstairs."

"I'm not afraid," I replied. "Besides, having anything unruly in the guest room doesn't fit in with your decor."

She and Alex laughed. We did not mention it again.

O

Although there was no more talk of the night visitor, that wasn't the end of it. As we were eating and chatting at the dinner table that evening, Lisa picked up the saltshaker in her right hand and gave it a few shakes—not above her food but behind her so that sprays of salt flew over her left shoulder. She casually went back to eating and talking as if it had never happened.

Alex glanced at his mom and then at me. I think he knew why she'd done it, but he didn't say anything. I pretended not to notice. I wondered if Lisa tossed the salt because of what happened in the guest room. *What does throwing salt mean?* It was not the right time to ask.

The idea of sleeping in the guest room again didn't bother me. Whatever roamed the room didn't come back to haunt me, and I slept through the night.

O

Lisa and I never spoke of the incident again. We continued to have our regular conversations at work—just as always.

After getting special permission, I searched the medical library for my type of experience. Science might call it a temporary state of paralysis, but that doesn't describe my situation. I was able to move throughout the entire event but decided it was safer to play dead.

Could I have experienced exploding head syndrome? This malfunction of the brain stem and spinal cord can cause a person to hear roars or bangs. Although I did hear two out of three sounds, what about the chains or the weight of the intruder? Would it be a syndrome if this only happened once?

People have had strange experiences with both positive and negative entities. The supernatural—shades, ghosts, hauntings, and possessions—all figure in religious literature, where nothing seems too weird to be included.

Alex and I didn't speak about the incident until about six months later. Lisa answered the phone when he called the office. Putting her hand over the mouthpiece, she said Alex wanted to talk to me.

After picking up the phone at the far end of the office, I nodded to Lisa, who hung up and helped a patient. "Aye, Alex," I said.

"Aye, Diana. Let me know if Mom picks up, okay?"

"I will," I said, wondering what was up.

"Did Mom tell you that two boys are staying at our house?"

Lisa had agreed to let two brothers named Aaron and Porter stay for a couple of months while their parents did missionary work. Alex said the boys had just let him and Lisa know they would not sleep in the downstairs guest room anymore. The creature came knocking, growling, and rattling chains, and when it jumped on the bed, they had run out of the room.

"Did it follow?" I wanted to know.

"No. It stayed in the bedroom," said Alex.

"What was it?"

"They said it was too dark. They just ran and didn't look back."

"Yes, it was too dark to see anything." I wanted to jump up and down. "Now do you believe me?"

"I always believed you because Rosie howled for no reason—right about the time you said it was there."

"How about . . ."

"Mom?"

"Yes."

"Mom did the same thing as before. We checked all the rooms. She told them it was the air conditioner. There was never anything wrong with it. Mom doesn't want to believe that thing is in our house, but she has to because it happened to Aaron and Porter too."

"That's the same creature—whatever it is—lion, bear, or monkey," I said.

Lisa stopped what she was doing and turned to look at me. I hoped she didn't just hear my end of the conversation.

"Your mom's almost ready," I told Alex.

"Okay—one more thing. You're braver than two boys. You stayed in the room. I thought you should know," said Alex.

"Thanks. I appreciate that." *More than you'll ever know.*

"If anything changes, I'll tell you."

"That sounds great. Bye, Alex."

Lisa picked up the phone.

It felt good. Finally—proof that it happened. I'm sure it's still there, but I never went back to experience it again.

A former classmate and his roommates once told me that

someone named Esa was looking for me. Esa? I've never understood why or how they were so sure about it either. I've never known anyone with that name, and I've never met another beast like the one who frequents Lisa's guest room. Since the creature didn't hurt me, I thought it would be perfect to humorously adopt it as my guardian. I gave it the name Esa since it was also looking for someone.

Whenever I need extra courage while walking on my own—especially at night—I imagine Esa can hear me through time and space. To call him, I'll knock, growl, and rattle my keychain, then say, "Esa, let's go for a walk. Nobody's going to bother me with you around."

Later, I learned that ESA is the abbreviation for an emotional support animal. Exactly. Well, maybe not exactly like my fierce guardian.

An intruder encounter is the last thing I ever expected to happen to me. Now, I wonder if it was a test of will and courage. I don't know if I passed, but the monster is now my protector.

6

WHALE

Under the influence of only the gorgeous weather, I decide to run some errands and drive the familiar Lawrence Expressway in Sunnyvale, California. There are fewer cars on the weekend, so I flow like water around any slow-moving impediments and plunge ahead to stay alert. The odometer is doing its job of recording the distance traveled as I watch the black asphalt until I'm unaware and blind to it . . .

An electric jolt combined with a jerking snap bring me back from the unknown, and I find myself driving on an unfamiliar part of the road. As I pass endless rows of allergy-producing bottlebrush and oleander bushes, I wonder if their pollen has caused me to drift off.

I check the odometer for some verification, but I get no relief from the reading. It shows I've driven more miles on the Lawrence Expressway than needed and missed my exit. This is troubling because it means I went into a trance even while speeding. It's unbelievable—my unconscious mind was driving the car. That's like using the back of my head to see the road in front of me.

There aren't any guide signs when I look in the rearview mirror. I try to recall the color of the last two stoplights. When I can't remember, it gives me a queasy feeling, like taking a bite of something and knowing it will not go down with a swallow. I force a long exhale through my mouth and begin focusing on my breath to relax and get the replay, but the memory of driving through those last few intersections has disappeared.

My worry goes to the worst possible consequences, and I see red lights in an imagined spread of bloody body parts from a collision caused by my white line fever. Uncomfortable knots of guilt reach my stomach. I try kneading away their pressure by sending lots of gratitude with a final *thank you* that I haven't killed anybody.

After a few big swigs from my jogger water bottle, I look for the next exit and think back to the first time this happened. It was when David and I were sixteen and inseparable. He was my first love. I'd just gotten my license and was driving his car while he sat next to me like a big brother. It wasn't the first time I'd ever driven it, so he already knew I could handle a larger car with a bigger engine.

We were on a stretch of highway in Northern Virginia, and the posted speed limit was fifty-five miles per hour. Just like today, the road was a continuous straight edge, not particularly crowded, and marked by evenly spaced broken white lines that whizzed by. Every move had been easy to negotiate. If the highway patrol had passed us, they would have noted a driver doing the speed limit, if they noticed at all.

Not long into our outing, I heard a distant tone coming through a tunnel. It was like being forced out of a deep sleep. My eyes were weighted down as they moved in the direction of the sound, which turned out to be coming from David.

In my veiled state, he looked like a shadow surrounded by a halo. My mind was too far away to comprehend anything through the haze. I couldn't make out what he was saying until his arm movements finally shifted my attention, and that's when I could hear him calling, "Diana, Diana."

I still wasn't alert enough to react to what was happening, so David had to grab the steering wheel. He avoided a highway construction crew working on the right shoulder with their cement truck parked in the slow lane. I was heading right for it until he swerved us out of the way.

"My God, Diana. You were staring like there was nobody home."

The reality of it sank in. My eyes weren't on the road, and I didn't even know it. "You saved us. I would've slammed us into that truck. We would have been killed instantly." My eyes were wide open like every bit of adrenaline in my body had surged into them.

David made eye contact with me before asking, "Did you know you were in some kind of hypnotic state?"

"No, no. I had no idea," I gasped. "I've never gone into a trance while driving until today. I didn't even know it was happening."

O

I gulp some more water and wish David were here now. I feel spooked because I don't know what caused this trance today. My law-breaking speeding strategy has always kept me vigilant, and so far, there's been no need to explain it in court.

When I see the next highway sign, I reconnect with my surroundings. I'm not at all where I'd planned to shop. I'm heading for the southern shore of the San Francisco Bay, as though I was guided here for some reason. My throat is still dry, so I pull over to fish for the water bottle that just rolled off my seat and onto the floor somewhere on the passenger side.

Giving myself a good talking to is what I call self-preservation. As I'm lecturing myself to wake up and stick my head in some cold bay water, a radio broadcast interrupts me. A male announcer reports, "A whale has been spotted swimming in the San Francisco Bay." The story makes me thirsty, so I gulp more water while I listen. He says it's a humpback whale and gives more details about its whereabouts like it's an unusual event.

The image of a swimming whale calms me down. I've been living in the San Francisco Bay Area just a few years, and the news of the humpback whale is intriguing because I've never heard about any whales traveling so far inland. Whale watchers go to the ocean to see these magnificent whoppers, don't they? I wondered if it had gotten off course like me.

Well, I can forget about running errands now. Annoyed with myself, I screech out of first gear, whip a U-turn, and head home. My emotional twister doesn't last long because my nature is 99.99 percent sunny.

Curiosity about that whale broadcast makes me the town crier, though. I call friends from school and work, telling them, "I heard a news story earlier about a whale that may be lost in the bay. When you hear it, let me know because the announcement sounded like it was a big deal."

Okay, I've barked enough. Someone's going to get the news and report back.

Tonight's entertainment plan is a movie with chips, guacamole, and margaritas. Casually dressed in jeans and shirts, Leila and I walk from our place to Portia's apartment. After taking off our boots for more comfort, we pad over to Portia's couch and slouch down in front of the TV.

I talk Leila and Portia into checking the news before the movie, but there's no story about a whale. They both turn to look at me. Portia wrinkles her nose while Leila just shrugs like she doesn't mind the slight detour in our plans.

"That was a big waste of time. I can't believe it. There was nothing about a whale in the bay," I say. Perceiving there's more explaining to do, especially because I mentioned going into a trance and passing my exit, I add, "The transmission was very clear. Anyone in the car would have heard it."

"Whales do make the news," says Portia, who isn't slow in handing out cocktail napkins. She grabs the pitcher of margaritas with a big chop-licking smile and fills our glasses.

"A whale has been spotted in the bay is how it usually gets

reported. Or we'll find out about a dead whale," says Leila, painting her fingernails a pearl color. After checking her skill, she blows on them and announces, "Let's have a toast to our lefty with a whale tale." She gingerly lifts her glass and beats Portia to the first sip, which has never happened before.

I'm thinking, *No whale, no toast*, but I go along and raise my glass too. I know I haven't made the whale story up. *Well, what else can I do but move on?*

Other friends, coworkers, and classmates report back in the coming days—there's no whale. They all tease me with fishy clichés.

O

Five months later, everyone's forgotten about the whale except for me. It's Halloween, and at the tech company where Portia and I work, we're encouraged to dress up. She and I keep our costume plans under wraps like some top-secret project. The radio transmission incident is my reason for making a whale costume of blue and green scales with sequin barnacles. The design is reversed: the whale tail is on my head, and the head is at my feet.

I'm already at work in costume when Portia arrives dressed as a yellow and black killer bee. Her short black wig glistens like the wings attached to her back.

"Turn around so I can see the details," Portia orders. She has me move slowly to show off how my costume is constructed. She frowns, asking, "Where are the eyes?"

"I ran out of time, so it's a blind whale," I say, giving an answer on the fly.

She fires back. "Well, we didn't see anything on TV about it, did we?"

I stick my tongue out at her. We both laugh and get back to observing people in their costumes.

"I've never had this kind of workday. It's like a party. I can't focus on my job," I whisper, almost forgetting to mention a wacky addition to my costume. "Watch," I say, and I squeeze and hold both cheeks together with my teeth to try and mimic a fish's mouth. "Since nothing on my face looks like a fish, this is what I'm doing."

Portia gives a thumbs-up. In her bee costume, she looks like she's all muscle, like a female boxer. Passersby laugh when she threatens to sting anyone who comes in her territory. "No biz working today. You know how we bees is." She buzzes and dances like a bee giving directions to some nectar.

"I can't speak with these fish lips." I end up making a fist and blowing into it to mimic a whale's loud, trumpeting sounds.

This winds up Portia. "Mizz motor mouth zee can't talk? Does zee fish haz zee lips?"

"Bee zee bee, look at these costumes. I'm going to grab my camera," I tell her.

It's hard to believe so many coworkers are into Halloween. These vampires, red devils, witches, cartoon characters, entertainers, political figures, and bloody zombies with sick gore all want group photos or portrait shots. Taking close-ups obscures a background of boring office decor, and if I'm lucky, lush green plants cover its blandness altogether.

Some of my coworkers know why I'm dressed as a whale. They find it funny, and I get teased all over again. A photo of me in my whale costume making fish lips ends up in the next month's issue of the company newsletter as a record of the event.

After Halloween, I put my costume away and stop thinking about the whale. Driving over the speed limit is still working to stop my trances, taking the stress off my mind.

O

It's almost one year later and time to design a new costume. After sewing it by hand, what's left to do is to insert wires into the black fins with silver sequins to turn myself into a lionfish for the exotic Halloween Ball in San Francisco.

The word is out to a few costume-creating girlfriends about dressing up for this year's photo caper around the San Francisco Bay Area. The first call back comes when I've just gotten to work.

It's Leila, who sounds excited. "Have you heard the news?"

After fumbling for my phone, I drop it on the desk. "What?" I give an embarrassed giggle. "Grr. I'm juggling the phone. What news?"

Leila spews her words. "There's a humpback whale in the San Francisco Bay. It's swimming the wrong way—away from the ocean and farther and farther into the bay."

When I give a little whoop of delight, Leila chuckles at the other end. "I don't care who heard that," I tell her. "Oh my—I don't have a god, and I have no sense of direction. This whale must be a relative."

Leila's laugh is muffled. "Right. You don't have a homing device," she says faintly.

"It's because I'm not from around these parts," I inform her, making my voice sound like a moaning whale.

She snorts, saying, "Aha, I knew there was something different about you. I must confess—I believe your whale tale. I just don't know how you heard the news years ago."

I try to explain. "It's like today jumped into the day I was living in nearly two years ago. Maybe going into that trance while driving had something to do with hearing into a future time frame."

"You are one weird girl. That would have scared me into thinking I'd lost my mind when the whale didn't show up. Sorry, I'm mumbling. It's called biscotti with coffee."

"Oh, that explains those muffled sounds," I say. "Do you want to get together after work? Let's celebrate when the whale story comes on."

Leila and I sit in front of the TV like it's movie night. When the whale appears as a top local news story, we cheer, and I feel vindicated.

Night after night, news of the whale continues. It's a male humpback whale, now called Humphrey. We watch him leap out of the water. His breaching creates a huge splash as his body hits the surface, and then he slides back under the waves.

This is turning into an unusual story, so we keep up with it. We're not the only ones either.

"What is wrong with this whale?" I ask.

"Maybe he's hungry or sick," Leila says. "But then he couldn't soar out of the water like that."

"Why are you swimming up the Sacramento River? You'll get into trouble." I turn my head left and right.

"Do you realize we've been following Humphrey's big adventure for a few weeks?" Leila blinks at me from under her long bangs.

"Yes, but I can't stop. I didn't get these details years ago. That broadcast didn't say anything about a dead whale," I tell her.

More weeks pass. The October weather in California has been clear and warm. Humphrey is still on the loose.

The front door slams. By the time I poke my head out of my bedroom, Leila's pulling off her jacket and has the TV remote in her hand. "Humphrey's one curious explorer, but he'll never find his mate in a river. It's on in a few minutes. Want to watch?"

"Yes," I say. "Just give a whistle. I'm reading something for class tomorrow."

Leila lets out a warble, then says, "One-minute warning."

"Okay. I'll read during the commercials!" I yell, racing to the living room with my textbook.

"It's worse. The teaser says Humphrey's stuck in the Sacramento River by a bridge." Leila's face looks tense and she's wringing her hands.

"Oh no. What can be done? There isn't much time!" I jump up and down, feeling anxious.

"What's he trying to do? Crawl out of the water to prove Darwin is right?" Leila asks.

"Yes, he's going to grow some legs and walk free. The whale's early ancestors had four legs and walked on land."

Leila's jaw drops. "Can you imagine? Is this what you're learning in physical anthropology?"

"Yes." It's too much for me to stay serious. "How about—it's going to grow into a handsome merman?"

Leila's dark curls swish as she moves her shoulders like she's heading to meet him. "Much better. Now you're talking." She giggles.

O

Day after day, the news gets more harrowing. The story isn't budging. The whale is still stuck.

Even with work and school, Leila and I stay on top of it. Everyone we know is too.

I'm not getting teased anymore, but I'm forever linked to a whale—and not just any old whale.

How Do I Know?

Leila and I are back in front of the TV. Before turning it on, I tell her, "You won't believe it. I heard a pylon is going to be removed from the bridge."

She stares for a few seconds before saying, "Now, that sounds impossible. Would human beings do this to save a whale?"

Although the pylon is removed to save the whale, Humphrey still isn't cooperating. "I don't want to look. I do want to look." Leila's voice chokes. "Must be a female thing." She sniffs.

"If I look at you, I'll cry too." I sigh and look out the window.

"Watch!" exclaims Leila. We watch as rescuers in small boats are closing in and banging pipes. "It's working. He's nearly corralled." Leila applauds.

"Yay. Humphrey may be heading out of there." I've been holding everything about his predicament in for weeks. "Finally. I can breathe," I announce, and I slump back down into the couch.

"I know what you mean," says Leila in a croaky little voice. "Imagine how the whale feels—like being an ET among humans."

After a month, Humphrey the humpback whale finally makes it back to the ocean. With all the angst in the world, this true tale has a happy ending.

My life has strange lessons. Thanks to Humphrey, I finally know how I heard that song on the way to the lake when I was fourteen—the song no one else in the car heard. Time shifted back to when this song was actually being played when I was alone. It's how I heard this news report about the whale ahead of earth's clock time. For some reason, time shifted ahead to the day the news was being reported, and I heard it on my car radio.

Why did I hear this whale's story? The American sleeping prophet Edgar Cayce once gave advice to a visitor while in a deep trance. He said, "Sometimes, an experience like this will be as a messenger. More time passing may reveal particular symbols and connections. Pay attention to these particular patterns internally and externally as guides."

7

THE NIGHT VISITATION

Dad waits for us in the doorway of his ranch-style home with the porch and path lights on. Behind his handsome frame and platinum hair, our house has the glow of a celebration. When my sisters and I arrive, we get his urgent news. "The hospital called," he says. "They want our immediate family to come as soon as we can."

Although we know what's coming, Dad's words are still a shock. Chase's eyes blink like she's asking a coded question. Dad responds to our younger sister like he's read her mind. "They won't tell us anything more."

"I'll wait for Josh to come home after work, and we'll go together," Chase offers. Helen and I both agree it's a good idea. Dad does too. We don't want our younger brother going to the hospital alone.

Uncle Robert sits in the front passenger seat. He's here to help with anything we need. I slide into the seat behind Dad and Helen sits next to me. Dad drives his new sedan at a good clip—most likely over the speed limit. We all notice, taking turns eyeing the speedometer, but nobody mentions it. The road ahead is as free and clear as the blue-black sky above the tree-lined highway. Endless foliage separates two lanes of sparse traffic heading in both directions.

Everything's as normal as it can be until I detect an odor from the hospital room. I know at once Mother has died and is now riding with us. I keep my awareness to myself.

Seconds later, Helen breaks the silence. "What's that smell?"

When no one answers, she leans forward to catch my attention. I turn to find her staring at me like I'm supposed to know. The control panel light reveals her beautiful face with her lips pinched tight like she doesn't dare say anything more. Helen twists strands of wavy dark blond hair through her fingers like she's making worry beads out of it.

"Hmm. I think it's our mother," I say, acting like I don't know for sure because I don't want to break the news. I wonder how Helen takes my remark, but we can't talk without Dad and Uncle Robert hearing us. When they don't say anything, she and I silently watch the road.

Flashing lights reflecting in the driver's mirrors and a tooting siren interrupt my thoughts. Without a doubt, this red and blue commotion is coming for us. *Who else is driving this fast?*

The uncanny timing makes my mind blare. *Did you help with this, Mother? I know you want to keep us safe, but you always worry whenever Dad drives over the speed limit. You can't ask Dad to slow down now, but you can influence things. You know what I mean. Dad is not going to get a ticket. I'm not going to let Dad get a ticket—not today.*

Dad signals as he slows down to pull off the road and onto the shoulder. Sure enough, the police car parks right behind us and the officer is heading for Dad's lowered window. My view from the back seat is part of the policeman's face, shirt, badge—and that's it.

I know I must be eye to eye to get this done, so I lunge for Dad's open window, squeezing my head and shoulders next to him like a contortionist. Helen grabs my belt and tries to pull me back in. She can't because I have one elbow wedged beside the headrest with the other one sticking out the open window like a pair of wings. Even so, it doesn't stop her from trying.

Dad doesn't get a chance to speak, and the policeman can't ask for his license or registration because I'm blurting, "The hospital called. We don't know if our mother is dead or alive."

The officer gives us a long, hard stare while our expressions say it all. "Go ahead," he finally says. "Drive carefully."

"Thank you, officer," I say, and I settle back in my seat.

This is the quietest car ride of my life, and I'm not talking about vehicle performance. We say nothing all the way to the hospital.

We're waiting when Chase and Josh come through the automatic doors. I notice our platinum-haired teenage brother looks a lot more like Dad now. Josh must have raced just like Dad to get here so soon after us.

Two days ago, he tried to prepare me by saying, "Don't be shocked by how Mom looks, sis." Then he put his arm around me as we walked to her hospital room. It was traumatic. At the sight of her, I burst into tears and so did she. Our family was lucky to have three more good days with her.

As Chase and Josh approach the reception desk, I hurry over. I keep my voice low, saying, "I have to tell you about an odor from the hospital coming into Dad's car. It was Mother. Helen and I both detected it, butI don't think Dad or Uncle Robert did."

"The same thing happened to us. A weird smell wafted into Josh's truck!" Chase exclaims.

"I don't doubt that it was Mom. She made the rounds then." Josh tucks his shirttail into his pants, adding, "It seems that only her children are able to smell her for some reason." Even though he's the youngest, his awareness is keen.

"I think so too," I say. "It's like Mother wants us to know that she's still here for us. I think she's trying to tell us there is no death—that we just drop the body and carry on."

"Now we know," Josh says. "Mom's still the teacher. What do you think about this, Chase?" He puts a supportive hand on her shoulder.

Chase glances up at him and gives his hand a squeeze. "We're lucky to get this information. It's a relief to know that Mother isn't *dead* dead. Thanks to her, dying isn't so scary to me now."

We hug and join the rest of our family in the hospital waiting room. When Helen and I hug, she whispers, "I knew that smell was

Mother too. I just needed someone else to say it."

"I understand," I tell her. Our eyes well up with tears and we both look away.

It's not long before Mother's doctor and the nurses who cared for her meet us in the waiting room. We receive the official news when the doctor looks straight at Dad and says, "I'm so sorry that I don't have good news for you. Your wife died this evening." Dad nods without speaking.

We are silent. The kind nurses who helped our mother for the last month of her life give their condolences. Although their news isn't such a shock because Mother visited to let her children know it first, our eyes tear and we bow our heads after hearing it.

After learning of Mother's formal status from the medical establishment, we're directed to follow the staff to her room. The hospital is a bleaker-looking place now. We pass bland walls and walk on ugly patterned linoleum floors. The monotonous hallways have a lackluster finish, and the harsh fluorescent lighting overhead mixes with it like an unsavory color palette.

Dad kneels at Mother's bedside and reaches for her hand. "I love her," he cries. That's it. We weep with him, unable to continue holding it in.

Mother must have heard us discussing odors. She has changed her scent from one of illness to the essence of her favorite flower. I bet she ran through gardenias—like taking a shower—because that's what we all smell now.

We can't see her, but whenever we get a whiff of gardenias in the house, we know she's here. When Dad feels her presence, he invites her to jump on the back of his bike, and together they go for a ride.

O

The day features a beautiful spring-green landscape and cloudless blue sky. I'm alone behind our house admiring the lush natural surroundings when I detect Mother leaving. She's within a soft rolling hum of a single chord of music—it's coming either from instruments or voices singing in unison. Maybe it's a combination of both, but I'm not exactly sure, so I walk in its direction for greater understanding. It's as if the sound opens a portal for Mother, who enters a dimension that's come just for her.

Back in California, my life isn't routine yet. No one is home when I decide to go out to the enclosed patio to sneak a smoke. Yes, a hush-hush smoke. While centered inside a slow, billowing exhale, I look down at the wedding rings Dad gave to me because I'm the eldest daughter.

The rings fit, but I feel guilty about wearing what belongs to my mother. A colorless diamond looks like crinkles of aluminum foil to me. But as direct sunlight hits its facets, mesmerizing colors appear, proving that this bright jewel has a practical use after all.

I try it out, and as I stare into each little sparkle, I wonder about my mother. Blind faith is never a satisfying option. What is death if no one really dies? To no one in particular, I demand to know where my mother went.

Since elementary school, I've had repetitive dreams of doors and getting through them. In these dreams, I float up to many kinds of doors, fancy or plain—even doors housing animals.

A door may have a feeling of sunrays, or a stormy force pounding with a mysterious energy behind it like the weather. When I'm in front of a door in a dream and then pass through it, day or night can be set to any time—past, present, or future—like entering a time machine.

In a recurring dream I've had since childhood, the closer I get to a particular door, the more it vibrates and shakes—almost bending to reveal a living light, like fire or something electric that glows in an unbroken pattern between the rectangular perimeter of the door and its frame. Being curious, my hand goes out, but I'm shooed away by elders before I can touch the door that draws me in. "You are not ready for this yet," their voices say whenever I reach for it.

The following morning, it's my first day back on the job since my mother's funeral. I have sunglasses and tissues by my side in case of an unpredictable blues attack. It helps that this office is in a back corner like a solitary hideaway.

I'm sitting behind my computer screen engrossed in work when I hear a voice. "Well, I'm not having any luck."

I lean sideways and see Portia in the doorway. A new haircut with long front layers softens her square face. With pleading brown eyes and her jaw jutting out determinedly, she looks like she's coming undone.

Uh-oh. This can only mean one thing—men. "Come on in. What's going on?" I ask.

Portia pouts like she won't talk, but she can't hold back. "I thought everything was fine. We don't have time to get into it here. I need a night out with my girlfriends. How about dinner tonight with Leila and me? I'm stuck and I really like this guy."

It's the end of the semester. My term paper, "Incest among the Higher Primates," is due for a physical anthropology class, but my professor has given me an extension.

Portia looks puzzled and then relieved when I say, "I don't have to be force-fed through the nose. Count me in."

We arrive at our favorite restaurant in Mountain View for the best chile rellenos around. Portia never wastes time ordering drinks and appetizers. She lets our waiter know what we want as soon as we're seated. Once our food arrives, she begins mysteriously. "I've been to three already."

"Oh? What comes in threes?" Leila asks, dipping a homemade tortilla chip in some salsa and guacamole.

Portia doesn't hesitate. "I've been to three psychics about my love life. I need some help."

Leila and I look at each other and grin. We know all about Portia's hunt for a husband. Extroverted, bright, talented, and willful—she's in a hurry.

Portia already knows that we have certain opinions, but she can't keep from asking, "What now? Why are you two grinning?"

"You know we have your best interests at heart. Just slow it down a bit. Your confidence is impressive, and so is the way you put yourself out there." I defuse her defensiveness before going after more delicious habanero salsa.

Leila leans back in her chair, and with a comedic quiver she spells, "R-e-l-a-x." She smiles. "That's right. Take it easy or you'll push the right one away."

This is not what Portia wants to hear. In frustration, she jabs at the ice with a straw after stirring her drink. "You're right. You're both right, but all my childhood friends are married. I'm the only one who's still single."

Here comes the bride. Make that run for your life. Run for your life. "You're only twenty-two. I don't understand the mad rush," I say. *What's the hurry?*

Leila's face is rosy from the tequila. "Oh, fortune tellers, my ass. Aren't they just cons to get your money?" She leans forward and points a finger at Portia. I expect her to wag it, but she puts her hand back in her lap.

I had the same opinion as Leila until finding out for myself that some fortune tellers are authentic. I shoot Portia a warning look. She referred me to a coworker who recommended Moriah, a psychic who gave me the best medical check of my life and other valuable information. I've kept it quiet.

After meeting Moriah, I had to throw out my erroneous opinions. The adorable, plump, gray-haired seer knew about my injured ribs and the scar on my knee. How? I was wearing jeans at the time.

Her medical check was superior to that of a lousy childhood doctor. "Eyes okay, nose okay, throat okay, ears okay?" That's what the doctor had asked without checking. Isn't he supposed to examine his new patient to find out?

I'd worn my mother's wedding rings to the reading and Moriah knew, even saying that I wasn't married. I hadn't expected her to mention it.

When Portia utters a single word, I return to my present surroundings. I hear her, but it doesn't click. "Michael, you say. It's Michael you're talking about?" I ask.

"No way. The Michael we know?" Leila's just as surprised.

"Yes, that's the one. We've been keeping it a secret for professional reasons." Portia takes a big gulp of her margarita and sighs as though revealing it brings some stress relief.

Michael is the assistant professor to Professor Tell, whose art class Portia, Leila, and I take a few nights a week. He's fun, talented, and a lot looser than our professor.

We're happy for Portia. Just the same, it doesn't stop us from turning into sisterly advice queens.

"Don't be pushy," says Leila, emphasizing every word. The way she makes them pop startles Portia and me.

"You've only known him two semesters. Be practical. Get to know the real Michael," I tell her.

Our advice doesn't deter her. With a sly, pouty mouth she asks, "How can I see him sooner?" Her fingers tap impatiently along the corner of the table.

"Well. There may be a way," I say.

"You mean something that won't be too obvious?" Portia stops her drumming.

"Yes. There's a Full Moon Sail event on the San Francisco Bay coming up. We'll invite Michael to come with us. Let's ask him and then get tickets."

"Sounds romantic," Leila says. "Maybe *I'll* meet someone there. Let's have a toast." When Leila lifts a petite arm, her fingernails gleam under the light.

Portia rocks back and forth, sloshing her margarita as she shoves her glass in the air, saying, "To your help and advice. I feel so much better now." Her nose wiggles with exuberance.

"Shine a magic moon—here we come. Cheers, truly," I say, dancing in my seat and waving my glass.

"How's your long-distance romance going?" Portia asks me. "It must be good—look at that ring. Are you engaged?" Leave it to her to spot a diamond.

"Still going. It's been six months now. No, we aren't engaged." A wave of sadness reaches my throat, making my eyes blur. I look down, saying, "I inherited this wedding set from my mother."

We're silent until Leila laughs. "Rings or no rings, all you have to do is flash those eyes."

Thanks, Leila. "What about my eyes?"

"You just have to twinkle those blue-green-golden eyes to have a partner on the dance floor whenever you want," she says, trying to cheer me up.

Recovering enough to make a goofy face, I say, "Like this? Will this get them to dance with me?"

Portia laughs and chokes on a tortilla chip—almost blowing it out of her mouth. She grabs for some water. "Argh. Silly girl."

"Oh, I get it. You're wearing those rings for protection until your East Coast boy comes out."

"Shh. You're giving away my secret." I chuckle.

"So, you two *are* serious?" Portia digs.

"Maybe," I say. "Well, yes. We're getting to know each other long distance. He's serious, but he's not pushing me. The truth is—I haven't met anyone that I like as much."

"So, it's your long-distance man, eh? Is he in your future?" Portia wiggles her eyebrows.

"I don't know about my future," I say, indirectly letting her know that I didn't ask Moriah about my love life. "I'm looking for a long-lasting relationship, but I need time to perceive if it'll work."

Leila nods her approval, settles the check, and holds up her to-go order for lunch tomorrow. "It's been fun as always. If Michael can't make it this weekend, do we want to go anyway?"

O

The October Full Moon Sail on the San Francisco Bay is romantic. Michael asks Portia out again right on the spot. She is a handful and that's okay with him. I love taking photos of everyone and plan to give copies as gifts.

Time has raced with packing and moving. Our night sail seems like yesterday, but it's the last month of the year. As college students, Leila and I don't have a collection of holiday decorations, but we can make something out of almost nothing to decorate our new home. She and her brothers find a large manzanita branch on the ground while hiking and manage to get it to our townhouse. We decorate it with small homemade ornaments and hang it from the living room ceiling hooks with fishing line.

"Heave-ho. One more box to unpack and we'll have a real living room. "This bathroom is perfect for my darkroom because it's the only room in the house without a window," I say, pushing the box of photography supplies around the corner into its new location next to the front door.

Leila fiddles with the pine cones I found while jogging. She adds a ribbon garland and tea light candles, moving them to the mantel while I unpack the last box in the bathroom.

She announces, "I'm already thinking about next semester." I groan, and she laughs. "What's that grumble? Did you finish that anthropology paper?"

"Yes, finally," I say. "But I had a near fiasco at work this morning and fought with the printer."

Leila's boots tap on the tile flooring in front of the fireplace as she works on her arrangement. "Is it still in one piece?" she asks.

"Ha ha. Not anymore," I joke. "Seriously, it got stuck in a weird glitch. After writing the final pages, I started the print job, but instead of my term paper, it printed symbols and codes, with few actual words."

Moving to the doorway, I explain, "The computer froze. So, I had to trick the printer into thinking it had completed its job to unfreeze it and save the file."

"I've gotten that screen freeze, but I've never had a weird printout. I turned off the computer and ended up losing everything I hadn't already saved," says Leila.

"I was desperate. Tricking the printer was all I could think of to do. It took time, though. I fed that printer like a paper-eating monster because I didn't want to lose what I'd written."

"Wow. I don't have that kind of patience. Just like I might lose my temper with this display if it doesn't come together soon," she says, whipping the red ribbon off the mantel.

"You'll make it beautiful," I assure her. "What a waste of time. Well, not a complete waste because I turned that used paper into merry mumbo jumbo tech holiday wrapping paper," I say, pointing to some packages on the couch.

Leila turns to see what I'm talking about. "Printer mishap wrapping paper—that's an original. Not a bad idea. I swear the printer is the weak link in the chain."

I make a tiny whistling sound and continue. "It doesn't stop there. With my paper ready to go, I jumped in my car, put my key in the ignition, and for some reason, the horn started honking on its own."

"Oh? That's bizarre. What'd you do?" Leila turns around to look at me after she cuts a few inches off the ribbon.

"I turned off the engine and kept hitting the horn until it stopped. The whole thing was unreal. I don't know if I stopped it or if it just stopped by itself."

"Lucky you," says Leila, placing the ribbon back on the mantel and weaving it around a line of pine cones.

"Yes, very lucky. By this time, being delayed by machines had me so mad that I started speeding toward the campus to meet today's deadline." My voice cracks a little. "I heard a siren, and the police car was right behind me. Can you believe it? We both pulled off the road. I was cursing and looking for my license when the siren blasted again. The officer pulled a U-turn and drove off, so I didn't get a ticket. All I could do was thank my mother and cry. Then I drove home."

I haven't talked about my mother until now. I choke up telling Leila about my dad driving us to the hospital, my mother's strange visit in our vehicles, and how he nearly got a speeding ticket on the way there. I stop talking when I can't hold back the tears anymore.

Leila consoles me. "It's okay to cry. You can talk to me anytime—I mean it. It'll help."

"I didn't want to walk around the campus upset, so I came home. I still haven't turned in my paper," I say between sobs.

"We'll take care of that. Let's go," Leila says, jerking the ribbon from the mantel again.

Her offer stops my sobbing. *Uh-oh.* Leila's a terrible driver who has no peripheral vision thanks to her dark mass of splendid curls. She drives under the speed limit and hesitates, and that makes me nervous.

Leila dislikes driving and I know it, so it's easy to persuade her not to. "I'll drive if you keep me company. I won't speed either. I promise." Like father, like daughter, like brother.

"Okay. I give up. Will you help me with the mantel arrangement when we get back? You're taller. Maybe that's why I just can't get it right."

"Of course. Once I drop off my paper, I'm free," I say, wiping the mascara off my cheeks.

By this time, it's late afternoon and the sky is thick with dark gray clouds. The light is easy on my eyes. As we head along, a flock of crows swirl overhead until a few make a sudden dive for the car, almost hitting it.

"Whoa, did you see that?" Leila puts a hand to her throat and pushes her hair back.

"That was close. Maybe the glass looks more like sky and less like a windshield," I say while fishing around in my purse for a barrette to help Leila keep the hair out of her face.

"Or it's feeding time, but there's no telltale bug splat on the windshield," Leila reports after leaning forward.

When we're stopped at a red light, I find the barrette and hand it to her. "Do you see any wind moving?" I ask.

"No. Only cars and birds." Leila deftly parts her hair on the side and clips the barrette near her right temple. "This works great. Thanks."

"It looks good," I say, and I accelerate at a gentle pace.

"When we get home, I want you to open your present. You'll know why when you see it," says Leila.

"Really? I can't wait. What's this car doing?" I have to move quickly to the right in my lane. Leila gasps at the near miss but says nothing.

We've cruised a short distance when three crows barely clear the windshield on the passenger side. Leila raises her arm defensively, exclaiming, "Eek! What's happening?"

"I don't know. It's like we're invisible or something," I say.

Another car swerves toward us, and this time, I'm able to get in the next lane. "I've never had this many near misses," I say, my foot shaking on the gas pedal.

Leila's hands are clenched. Her voice wavers. "I'm glad you're driving."

"Me too," I whisper under my breath. Then I announce, "I'm turning my lights on even though it's not dark yet."

"Good idea," says Leila, fidgeting with her rings.

"Things have been on a weird roll since I got up this morning. A kind of odd warping is going about that's hard to describe," I tell her as I pull into the campus lot and park. "Yay. I'm going to beat that deadline—barely. What a load off."

"Congratulations. I'll just wait here and relax for a minute," Leila says.

There's something unusual in the air today. It's like the Mystery Spot in Santa Cruz, California, just moved down the mountain into Silicon Valley. Maybe things will start rolling uphill next.

O

Our drive home is unremarkable. We're back at the mantel positioning pine cones, tea light candles, and ribbon. "If we stand in the doorway, we can see how it looks with the manz," says Leila, using her nickname for the manzanita branch. We agree everything looks great and call it a night.

"Thanks for the perfect present. This space heater will get lots of use," I say, grabbing it. We head upstairs, telling each other of our plans for the weekend. "Oh. I'm also meeting Jeremy after work on Friday. That's tomorrow," I add.

How Do I Know?

After a jog and a Friday night dinner with my friend Jeremy, I get home. It feels colder inside this old California townhouse than outside. It's not insulated, and the windows aren't sealed. The heat's not efficient either; it warms the downstairs but not the second floor, so we turn it off at night.

The house is dark and Leila's not up to chat with, so I go upstairs to my room. Opening the door, I get a blast of cold air. As I hit the set of switches on the wall, the lights glow with such a welcome that I stop to admire my new bedroom.

The clock on the nightstand shows it's just after ten. *Wings*, a large watercolor I painted in honor of my mother, hangs above my bed and is the room's focal point. Art objects and photographs are displayed around books on a tall bookcase, and there are some personal creations too.

Feeling happy with my room, I walk in, and just as my foot crosses the threshold, the digital alarm clock goes berserk. As though synchronized with my entrance, it starts flipping through time. Hours shorten and days of the week fly into the future. I've never seen the time on any clock swing around crazily by itself.

This is strange. The lights are working fine—so what's wrong with my clock?

I resolve not to bother Leila to discover if the power went out earlier. Besides, my clock would've been blinking twelve o'clock if it had. I reset the time and it's back to working fine.

My bedroom is the larger one, as it has an en suite bathroom.

Leila didn't want it, but I'm happy to have it since there's more wall space for art. It does get colder because of the extra windows, and that's why Leila bought me a space heater.

I decide to take a hot shower. Heat, steam, and the scent of Bee & Flower soap deliver their comfort. I shiver like an electric toothbrush even in flannel pajamas, which helps me brush my teeth faster. I giggle about vibrating like an appliance as I lean back against the vanity to check the long horizontal window eight feet above me. There's a definite draft coming in from someplace.

This is a wintry night all right. Once I'm in bed, something rustles in the stillness, changing the quiet. No devices are on, but there's the feel of a voluminous atmosphere.

A subtle murmur makes the mm-mm sound of a fly grazing an ear—only nothing has flown by. It must be coming from outside. I hop out of bed, making sure both windows are closed. Although the nearby trees are still, their branches lit by streetlights, I sense a swirling like leaves gathering and lifting into a funnel of wind.

A second survey of the room confirms that objects on the bookcase, dressers, and nightstand don't need rearranging. My big watercolor, *Alien with a Mask* hangs level in its frame on the opposite wall. Sleepily, I reach for the lamp switch and turn it off.

The new space heater glows orange like a real fire. It's positioned next to the side of the bed—just close enough to be safe. It stays on, but the room doesn't feel any warmer from its constant heat.

Usually, I fall asleep within a minute or two, but not tonight because my feet are cold. I rub my long legs together like I'm trying to get two sticks to smolder.

My eyes are closed until there's a dawning in my mind. It's not just a cold night. The circling draft creating a breeze is bringing in something more than whatever caused my digital alarm clock to behave erratically.

Whispering people are approaching within the night's slight wind. I sense the gravity in the tone of these voices, and there is a weightiness to this secretive blob of minds. Speech without a human voice box fills the bedroom like the presence of an invisible fog, becoming as thick and heavy as a wave.

These aren't like the visitors who first presented themselves to me when I was four years old. I'm not sure how to perceive them, but I'm not afraid.

As I sense the different essence of this group, the pace of their chatter starts to quicken as though they can't stay long. When a strange kind of upload of information begins, I pick up a pen and a small pad of paper from the nightstand and start writing.

Curious impressions come to me, including the face of a male stranger. Images appear along with geometric shapes that are interspersed with snippets of words. Like a reporter, I jot, draw, fill, and flip through many pages.

While writing, I get the sensation of a tempest building, and as its force grows stronger, the temperature suddenly drops. It feels as though I'm inside something like the positive, light area of a yin-yang symbol. The realm around me is the opposite of that—gray to black—mostly negative and dark.

This is what I'm starting to grasp. It's like being in the eye of a rising storm of consciousness that has a physical aspect to it.

When I can't get warm under the covers, I decide to get out of bed. I feel the heat as I kneel closer to the space heater with my elbows propped up on the bed. Still, I'm trembling from the frigid air.

As I inch over to the heater's glow, wondering how close is hazardous, an uneasy feeling washes over me, turning into something I've never felt before. I shudder with absolute fear, and my entire nervous system goes into high alert, with the hairs on my arms standing up like sentries ordering me to move.

My speeding pulse screams at me to run. As I fight this dead-end thought to control my rapid breathing, dread strikes with a quickening in my chest, making my heart pound. Something is coming up behind me.

It enters through the bedroom door, moving silently along the wall, heading in my direction. With my spine shaking, I force myself to turn around. My eyes land on the pewter butterfly frame surrounding a small mirror that leans against some books six feet away.

When the force approaches the bookshelf, I freeze right where I am. My beautiful butterfly mirror now reflects the male head of a red devil with horns. I sense coldness, no heart, and no conscience as it creeps behind me like a silent shadow. It goes by like this is Passover. Although this image shocks me, I don't fight it or run away. As soon as this face disappears from the mirror, I feel warmer.

How Do I Know?

I don't hallucinate. Although I don't believe in the devil, I'd be lying if I said its appearance wasn't terrifying.

When I scramble into bed and pull the covers up to my chin for warmth, something follows me. I sense a group surrounding my bed who are trying to get me to side with them. What I mean is that it feels as though they are literally trying to turn my neck all the way around. It is a grotesque feeling, like scenes from George Orwell's book *1984*. The group's consciousness is human, but there is a nonhuman element like a machine here too, and it's fast.

There is some strange communication related to five or fifth. Fifth generation—that's what I detect from it. Being the fifth generation of college-educated family members is the only fifth that makes sense to me personally. I can't figure out what fifth the group is talking about, but I'm sure they aren't referring to a fifth of alcohol.

I don't understand why these night visitors are here. What do they want from me? I would never agree with them. Again, I don't fight—I am just an observer trying to perceive the meaning of this event. I also wonder if it can or will kill me because its energy is pushing with the strength of a tsunami.

Does this mean I should prepare for death? As I worry, the familiar hospital smell enters, and I know my mother is now in the room with me. I feel her force right above me from head to toe. She acts as a shield protecting me from the chaotic onslaught of this darker negative area of consciousness.

My mother educates me about those in the room and their communication. She does it by having me look at the TV screen, of all things. She projects her thoughts, and even though the television is off, its screen suddenly turns an ugly dried-blood shade of red. I understand what she is transmitting to me. It's a description of what is here in the room with us. The notes I've taken are straight from their communication—the real scoop. My mother is counseling me to know the difference.

I trust her pitch-perfect warning and get a mother's protection from beyond the grave. She must have some influence because there's a shift, as though some settlement has occurred, and the group lets me go. They don't kill me, but maybe they have in another time, in another body. Mentally, it's like I've already died in some way, or maybe I understand death now through my mother.

After this trial or test, the feeling of being in the positive, light inner area of the yin-yang symbol's nuclear core strengthens. For hours, I focus on it to avoid being sucked into the larger, negative outer area.

Under the covers it's still cold and I turn from side to side. The steady glow of the space heater illuminates the patterns of the artwork on the wall. To my relief, nothing more appears in the mirror or on the TV screen as the night goes on.

My mother guards me like she wields the powerful shield of the goddess Athena. The force and fill of the visitor consciousness can't get past her loving protection. Maybe I've learned a little bit more about how to protect myself by not fighting and staying light.

Well, I did ask. I demanded to know where my mother went when she died. Now I've crossed this threshold and connected to a powerful dimension that heard me, found me, and replied by trying to swallow me whole. It's the strangest experience of my life. I hope to make it through this initiation alive.

When the first glimmer of sunlight appears, it comes in like a revelation. *I'm not going to die.* As though revolted by a sunray, the negative single-group entity consciousness flows back through the portal to its dimension.

I've never been so relieved to see daylight, and I brighten with the rising sun. Gone is my ethereal mother before I've had a chance to thank her.

After dressing, I head downstairs with the yellow mini legal pad full of notes. A cup of coffee gives me enough coherence to review everything I wrote. After a second cup, leaving plenty more for Leila, I head outside with my mind made up to burn all of it.

The car's frosty windshield confirms it was a freezing night. I opt for a walk to the nearby woods with my hands curved over the pad of yellow papers. Matches are tucked into the pockets of my winter coat. Hanging from my shoulder is a harnessed jogger water bottle swinging along with my movements. I hike the trail at a quick pace, blowing frosty dragon-cloud breaths ahead of me.

Pushing through thick, camouflaging shrubbery, I reach a secluded area of trees off the path and find a large eucalyptus tree. To honor my mother, I kneel at the base of its trunk to push away bark, leaves, and twigs with my bare hands, making a safe clearing of dirt in the shape of a circle on the ground in front of me.

I thank my mother for her guidance and protection as I tear out the pages. I strike a match to light the first page and then use it to light the next page. I control the fire by tamping the flaming paper edges into the bare dirt. Reviewing the transmission doesn't bring back any distress—only what I've learned.

The fire ritual has me so focused that I'm startled by a voice asking, "Mommy, what's that girl doing?" Peering through the foliage is a little girl in boots and a hooded jacket. She's pulling on her mother's hand, encouraging her to see for herself.

With pages left to burn, I ignore them until my honoring task is finished. To make sure no live embers remain, I sprinkle water on the bare area in a tight spiraling pattern and double-check the burn area.

Now the mother is kneeling next to her daughter and they're watching me. When I give a friendly wave, they both smile and wave back. Lowering my head to look busy, I take a few moments to reflect on specific past events as they relate to my present experience.

My elders kept shooing fearless young me away from certain doors, and now I know why. Some of the door dreams were dress rehearsals training me to handle the powerful dimensional reality behind them. Thank you for this experience. Thank you, Mother, for protecting me. I love you.

The mother and daughter continue their walk in the woods. I wait until they are out of sight and head home.

There's no sign of interference now. It's as though everything about that realm disconnected from this dimension and moved elsewhere, taking its weird effects with it. Membranes, bubbles, wormholes, and tunnels—how does it zero in on its target, open, close, and exit? Did my mother enter my room by reversing the way she left this world?

When I come through the front door, I greet Leila's reflection in the large dining room mirror. It's like the kind you'd find in a dance studio. "Today's a cold beauty," I tell her.

"Just in time." She smiles because she has all the ingredients for a salad and portobello mushroom sandwiches spread out on the kitchen counter.

I help her with the salad and set the table while she grills the mushrooms. We sit down to eat in the open-concept kitchen and dining room.

"It was freezing last night and there was frost on my windshield this morning," I tell her.

"My heater was on. After working overtime, I went to bed early and slept in," says Leila, reaching for the pepper shaker.

"I'm grateful for that space heater. My room was drafty, and I tossed like my neck was being turned around."

"Hmm. Maybe you need a new mattress with more support." Leila pushes a sliding portobello back inside her sandwich.

"That's a thought. Well, it was a wild night."

"Oh? If there was a storm, I missed it." Leila hands me the salad dressing.

"My night was like our drive to the campus. Instead of swerving birds and cars, the room was full of something like weird weather." I glance at her and pour some dressing.

Leila stiffens like she did when those crows flew at the windshield. "Are you telling me this house is haunted?"

"No, but my mother visited me last night," I say, almost holding my breath.

"Really visited? Or was it a dream?" She already knows about my mother visiting our family after she died. She didn't express disbelief over it.

I swallow a large bite to continue talking. "Not a dream. I was wide awake when she visited. It's the truth."

Leila looks doubtful as she skewers the vegetables in her salad like she's making a small kebob. "But your mother is dead," she says.

"Yes, but that doesn't mean she no longer exists. Apparently, she can still visit, like I told you."

"So you saw her last night," Leila says, taking a little bite of her sandwich.

Well, she's still eating. That's a good sign. Leila was scared enough to move because she saw a ghost standing behind her when she was brushing her hair in the bathroom mirror one night.

"It wasn't like the ghost of the old lady you saw in that apartment you rented before we met. I didn't see my mother, but I smelled her like before. She protected me from something like a storm in my room."

"Is she haunting you?" Leila gives me an uneasy look.

The idea of my own mother haunting me is funny. "No, my mother isn't haunting me—it's nothing like that." I try not to smile.

"I'm having trouble understanding what you're saying." Leila looks confused. "What do you think was in your room?"

"What visited me last night isn't easy to describe, but nothing's in my room now. If you like, we can go look so you can see for yourself."

"I'm getting creeped out," says a wide-eyed Leila.

"Whatever was there didn't hurt me. There's no need to worry because it's gone and so is my mother." I try to reassure her.

After loading the dishwasher, Leila tells me her plans. "I'm dropping off presents at my parents' house. Then I'm going to a movie with my brother and his girlfriend." A line forms between her eyebrows as she stares at me before asking, "How are you doing?"

"I'm fine. Really. I'm going to have fun working in my darkroom."

A little later, I hear her boots tapping closer to the front door. It closes as I'm selecting the first photo to print.

This townhouse may be old and cold, but I love having my own darkroom. Under the red safety light, I'm thrilled as the first image appears in the developer solution. When the timer rings, I grab the print with tongs and slide it into a stop bath to halt the development process. Once it's been in the fixer tray a few minutes to set the image, I admire the wet photo before dropping it into a final water bath.

After enlarging and processing my favorite black-and-white photos of Portia, Michael, and Leila in costume wearing wild makeup on our night sail, I store the negatives in plastic sheet protectors. I think about last night as I hang the wet photos to dry on a makeshift clothesline. *Who wouldn't be excited to experience a different realm?*

I get back to the reality of cleaning up the darkroom when a color video of Jeremy coming to visit me begins playing. It has a vivid real-time quality just like seeing it live, so I want to know if it's real or just my imagination.

Since my darkroom is next to the front door, I can verify what I just saw. I open the door to find Jeremy standing there with his arm up, ready to knock. He looks at me in surprise because his fist is about to connect with my grinning face.

Ha ha. This is the best thing to happen to me since last night.

I press both hands to my cheeks and say, "You are not going to believe what just happened." He stands there looking amused by my animated hand gestures. "I saw you with my mind's eye!" I exclaim.

"Really." Jeremy makes it sound more like a statement than a question. He looks at me in his unflappable way, like this kind of thing happens every day.

"Yes," I say excitedly. "I was finishing up in the darkroom when my mind just lit up like a remote camera and I saw you walking up the sidewalk to the door. It looked so real that I had to open the door to see for myself—and it was real."

If Jeremy's surprised, he doesn't say anything. Maybe he already knows the mind can operate in this way. Even though I've never had this kind of peculiar experience, I decide to say nothing more about it. I wonder if it's a perk from last night.

He just gives me another one of his unreadable stares and apologizes. "I was thinking about you. I should have called first, but I took a chance that you might be home. If it's not a good time, let me know."

Dressed like he's still on the job, Jeremy's wearing a white shirt with gray pinstripes, no tie, and gray trousers, even though it's Saturday. "I'm taking a break from this thing I have to do for the president and marketing heads," he says.

I chuckle at his choice of words, calling his strategic research job "this thing." I say, "The research part is interesting, but whenever it's math, I'll doze off."

"You're good in math—I can see it in your art," replies my math-whiz friend.

"Well, this is a first." I blush in disbelief at the compliment.

Jeremy is still standing in the doorway because I haven't invited him in. Before I do, his face lights up. "Say. Would you like to go out for some coffee and a sweet treat?"

Going anywhere with him is a guaranteed adventure. "I would, and your timing is perfect because I was up all night due to something unbelievable. I told Leila, and well, she didn't understand me." I know I sound disappointed.

"Try me. By the way, here's a present for you." Jeremy reaches in his back pocket and pulls out a pack of socks. "For jogging."

"What a presentation." I laugh. It's unconventional and just like him. "Thank you. I do need some of these. You're trying to get me into full jogging attire, aren't you?"

He just smiles. "I've found a great place I think you'll like. We can talk there."

O

When Jeremy drives, there's no weird atmosphere and no warping. "This is it," he says, parking at a coffee shop with a flower shop and greenhouse next door.

"You always find remarkable-looking places," I compliment him, surveying the coffee shop's dark gray exterior with its large-paned windows and incredible arch over the patio area. At the entrance are two unadorned stone urns, each containing a miniature evergreen and spilling ivy vines. "It's beautiful," I say, touching the ivy.

"I thought you'd like it." Jeremy's eye for the unusual is what I love about him. Quirky adds some mystery. I'm still ogling the arch when I hear him say, "It's even better inside." He holds the door open. I giggle with embarrassment over taking so long.

Everything else disappears when I see the mural art. The painted walls are a wild mix of dance movements that would have been right at home in my bedroom last night. I'm immersed in it when a wonderful aroma brings me back enough to say, "What a one-of-a-kind place. It took a lot of effort to pull all of it together."

We find a tall booth reminiscent of an old train carriage. Fidgeting to get comfortable, I fiddle with my long hair until it hangs in front of me like a tail. Once we've given our order, I lean back against a puffy headrest. "Ah, this is it." I sigh. Jeremy sinks back in his seat, closing his eyes like he's taking one of his famous power naps.

Our eyes pop open when our waiter says, "You're in luck. We just pulled our green chile apple pies from the oven."

The scent of coffee makes us sit up straight. "Mm to this double mocha," I say with whipped cream sticking to my upper lip.

Jeremy sips his latte and murmurs, "Try the pie."

"Wow," I say after taking the first bite. "I love it," I mumble, enjoying the zing of heat from the green chile.

"It's how they make it in New Mexico. The mural art is really something, isn't it?" Jeremy looks at me intently.

"The dancers' costumes are so brilliant and eye-catching that my imagination went dancing off."

Jeremy's face flashes with enjoyment as it does whenever he's treated me to something new. "It's unusual for a coffee shop to have such quality mural art. This female artist was commissioned by the owner."

"I can see why. Her art is magical. Thanks for bringing me here. It's cleared away a sleepless night."

Jeremy's cup obscures his mouth as he takes a gulp, but the crinkling corners of his eyes give away his smile. Before telling him about last night, I decide to ask a few questions first.

"Do you know that Jonah and the whale story?" I ask. He nods. "How about the Greek myth where Hades snatches Persephone and takes her to his underworld?" I get another yes. "Did you ever read George Orwell's *1984*?" He nods again.

Jeremy's gaze is intense. "I've been trying all my life to experience the deeper meaning of these stories," he says.

Wow, I think. "I thought you'd understand," I say, sighing with relief. "Last night, it was like parts of these stories came to life. It's not easy to describe."

In response, Jeremy leans all the way across the table and reaches for my hands. He holds both gently in a show of support before letting go. Thanks to his encouragement, I continue.

"A few days ago, some kind of chaotic time-warping interference came into my life." I describe what happened with the printer, my car horn, and the digital clock.

His expression remains unchanged when I recount the wild drive to the college campus with Leila. "She witnessed it," I say. "I told her it came to my bedroom, and so did my mother, who protected me. Experiencing it while in a human body is hard enough. Trying to explain what happened is worse because it's like an alien event with a language I don't know." I give another sigh, adding, "What I told Leila scared her. Now I get the feeling she thinks I've gone mad. By the way, I'm just as sane as the last time you saw me."

Smiling, Jeremy asks, "Do you know the story of Buddha under the Bodhi tree?"

"No, but I'd love to hear it." Listening to one of Jeremy's stories will give me a chance to relax and ground myself in the moment.

After taking a sip of coffee, he says, "Buddha was shielded by an entity known as the mighty serpent that protected him from the realm of chaos as he sat beneath a Bodhi tree. It sounds like your mother protected you by shielding you in the same way. I believe she really was there along with everything else."

Boosted by his belief in me, I say, "Buddha's experience does sound like mine. I'm not crazy either. It really happened."

"No, you're not crazy. You're just living it. I think you are the temple."

Whoa. I wouldn't go that far. I chuckle at Jeremy's statement about being a temple. "Well, I'm still me," I inform him.

He looks amused, telling me, "Oscar Wilde, the Irish poet and playwright, said, 'Be yourself. Everyone else is already taken.' It's a favorite quote of mine."

"That's clever!" I exclaim, giggling.

"You're doing fine. Let's talk more once I've finished this

strategic project. What does your jogging schedule look like this week?"

"Wide open. I thought you'd never ask," I tease.

Jeremy surprises me by asking, "Do you want to check out the flower shop before we head back?"

"Yes, if there's enough time." When he extends an arm in its direction, I say, "Oh, I didn't miss that beauty."

The flower shop is beautiful on the inside with a nursery of healthy plants and young trees. We stroll past stained glass, wind chimes, tools, colorful pots, and garden statues. When we reach the flowers, Jeremy says, "Pick anything you like to make a big, big bouquet." He opens his arms wide to show how big.

My nose leads me to the freesias. "I love their fragrance, so I'll start here." I pick them first.

"Among my favorites too," Jeremy responds.

After selecting some ranunculus and delicate greenery for a woodsy-looking bouquet, I gravitate to unfamiliar blooms. "Do you know these blue slipper-like flowers? I'll get a few and that's it."

What I've picked ends up looking like a small wedding bouquet. "Are you sure you don't want to make it even bigger?" Jeremy encourages me, but I shake my head because he'll have to buy a vase too if I make it any larger. The shop owner takes note and offers to arrange everything.

Jeremy gives his approval and then guides me back to the blue flowers, saying in a hushed voice, "The name of the flower you asked about is blue monkshood. You've reminded me of a good friend—an extraordinary mathematician and monk. One day, I dropped by for a visit and found my friend writing some extremely complicated mathematical formulas. As he explained them, I tried to understand him, but the math was way beyond my comprehension. He said an invisible force conveyed the formulas to him through his stereo speakers."

This intrigues me greatly and I ask, "May we visit your friend? I'd like to meet him and compare our experiences."

Jeremy's answer is even more of a surprise. "We can't."

The story of his friend is too curious to drop, so I prod gently, saying, "I'm going to ask a personal question. If you don't want to answer it, I won't be offended. Why can't we see him?"

"He wasn't able to handle the power of his experience." Jeremy's answer stuns me.

"What happened to him?"

Jeremy gives me a wistful look. "He was never the same afterward. He hasn't regained his sanity to this day."

"Maybe I can talk to him," I offer.

"It's not possible," he says, looking downhearted in a way I've never seen before. Then he reveals, "Some Buddhist sects try to bring on this experience."

He pauses to stare at me for a moment before explaining. "The head monk tells his students to choose somewhere to stay as they go for a walk with him—at the trunk of a tree, in a ravine, or in a cave. He goes home, but these initiates must stay in place overnight until he comes back the next day. It's not uncommon for him to find a few of them dead because this force is a real thing. You're right—it's not easy to negotiate when in a human body."

The seriousness of Jeremy's information startles me. For the first time, I understand how innocent I am because the possibility of going mad from my own encounter never occurred to me. I was more curious than scared, and I was never frightened enough to die there on the spot, even though the experience itself *is* like a death. It's always my way to give a grateful thank you when I'm helped with the impossible by the inconceivable, like receiving my mother's protection last night.

I'm so humbled that I lower my head to pull myself together before I can tell him, "Thank you for being here. Everything you've said means so much to me. And I feel very lucky to be spoiled by the coffee shop treats and these special flowers."

Jeremy's smile returns. "Just some early presents for my favorite jogger."

The moments I spend with Jeremy are important, and I wonder if he's the wisest man in the world. I don't know about his mind, but mine shifts into areas that I didn't even know existed when he's around.

O

A few days later, there's a knock at my front door. Standing in the doorway is a man in a police uniform who introduces himself. Someone called, worried about me.

It's the busybody across the street. She annoys everyone in the neighborhood, including her own family.

The policeman and I talk some more, and then I find out. Yes, the call is about me. Did Leila instigate his visit because my poor explanation put her fear factor over the top? I don't know and I don't ask. But the caller has provided an unexpected and unusual opportunity.

Right now, I have two choices. I can invite the policeman in, prove my sanity, and watch him leave, or I can go with him to find out what determines insanity. How else can I get behind padded cells with locked doors?

I don't care who phoned the authorities about me. I know I'm not crazy. They think I've been sane all my life and gone bananas a second later—really? How does this make sense?

The policeman isn't saying that I have to go with him. He isn't demanding anything. He seems to leave it up to me.

I want to find someone who's had an experience like mine. I could meet someone like Jeremy's monk friend or have a practical educational adventure without sitting in a classroom. In the end, the story of Jeremy's monk-mathematician friend influences my decision.

The policeman and I walk side by side to his black car parked out front. He opens the back passenger door for me. Missing door handles on either side are a surprise. This means I'm in for good and in his care now.

"Call me Jim," says the policeman, who is probably in his early thirties. Since he's from the East Coast too, we have fun talking about West Coast differences.

I don't ask where we're headed. Instead, I turn around to read the green highway sign we've just passed and notice a familiar-looking blue car behind us. I'm surprised when I see Leila driving and Portia sitting in the passenger seat. *Well, now I know.* I smile and wave. They wave back and then look at each other.

Jim and I arrive at a nondescript gray building with unreachable windows. He lets me out, saying he's enjoyed our conversation. We wish each other a Merry Christmas and Happy New Year before he leaves.

Here's where I'll find out what's sane or insane. But I'm wrong.

This place is a hub—like a dingy bus terminal with an attached office building. I fill out forms in the circular waiting room where many other people are seated. Everyone looks normal, presentable, and well behaved. Even though a juggler-magician decides to sit next to me and show off, it's a long wait.

Finally, I'm summoned to the front desk. A male and a female with tan uniforms and badges escort me to the other side of the garage. We stop in front of an ambulance. *An ambulance?* They open the back door, pull out a gurney, help me onto it, and strap me in. Then I'm pushed back into the vehicle and the rear doors are closed.

This is different and, to put it bluntly, even a bit crazy. Now I'm in restraints like I'm having a medical emergency. There's nothing to do but stare sideways at traffic or up at the beige ceiling.

How Do I Know?

The paramedics get in the front compartment and turn the emergency lights on. We aren't flying down the road. We are a slow-moving nonemergency just as stuck in rush hour traffic as everyone else. The beacon lights flash on the windows of the surrounding cars.

Periodically, the paramedics turn around and apologize for the long trip. I acknowledge them with a smile and say nothing. I'm not hysterical or complaining about being restrained, so I wonder why they keep checking on me. It isn't like I can unstrap myself and escape like Houdini.

Thanks to the stop-and-go traffic, it takes us close to two hours to arrive at our destination. At last, we enter another garage, and the medics open the back door of the ambulance. My calm sunniness must throw them because they look closely at me. For what? Signs of craziness? *Eek. Guess what—I'm not crazy.*

Although I can't see where I am, I assume this place is a real mental institution. I'm still in restraints when the dim garage lighting shifts to an intense glare as I'm wheeled through two sliding glass doors and parked in front of what looks like a brightly lit command center with its guards and staff now eyeing me.

First, I'm handed off to the staff and the necessary paperwork is verified. When the medics leave, the doors lock behind them and there is no way to escape. Now I'm in their fishbowl.

Although the medical staff and guards observe me closely, I'm not bothered, violent, belligerent, combative, or drooling. I follow their instructions and answer or ask questions. After deciding that I'm not a threat to the other residents, they untie me.

I assume this interview and meeting the other patients will take a few hours, but I'm wrong. Instead, they tell me I'll be here for three days. *What? Days?*

I'm hungry and it isn't too late to eat. What I choose from the cafeteria gets delivered to me in the rec room down the hall. It's a large room painted neutral gray with cheerful posters and info on the walls. Nothing looks like holiday decor.

My food arrives and tastes like a TV dinner. I observe while I eat. There aren't any females here, and the men appear to be in various degrees of sanity. Most of them are young. A few have beards, more are conservatively dressed, and some look like bikers. *Who has what?* I can't answer my question until I have more time to assess them.

Once I finish eating, it's time for a shower and bed. I've come to the institution with nothing—not even a purse. I find the shower area on my own. It's large enough for six people and reminds me of a gym locker room. Like swimming in the wild, I wash and groom without any toiletries. There are no obvious monitors, and for a mental institution, there seems to be plenty of freedom of movement.

After putting my same clothes back on—underwear, jeans, sweater, and boots—I walk alone to my assigned room. I should have just run down the hall hanging on to the tiny towel and carrying my clothes because now I end up taking everything off again. *Well, I probably would have been chased for inappropriate behavior*, I think as I fold and place my belongings on a metal chair before jumping into bed naked.

The next day, I meet with the psychiatrist in his office. I'm wearing my same clothes. He asks a few general questions—name, age, and why I think I'm here.

How can I possibly sum up my experience without a universal vocabulary? "The world," I say. I begin with these words because it's like another kind of world came into my bedroom.

The psychiatrist lowers his head and looks down his nose at me. He parrots my words in a rote manner, turning them into a drawn-out question. "The world?"

I know he doesn't have it in him to understand my experience. It's hard enough for me to describe it. So, there can be no real discussion.

This doctor is not patient friendly. He has no bedside manner, and oddly, he's almost devoid of personality. I wonder how he got the job. His dull tone of voice and flat affect are enough to put someone to sleep.

I decide to stick to the mundane—something familiar to him. "My mother passed away," I tell him. This sounds normal enough. My dead mother coming back to protect me during a visitation by half of the yin-yang symbol or consciousness with its force and prophecy is not something to mention. It would open cans of questions begging for labels.

The psychiatrist seems burned out. He doesn't care when he asks, "Are you depressed?"

"I'm grieving," I answer. "The blues come and go." So that he doesn't think I'm immobilized, I say, "Despite my grief, I'm working full time. I'm on semester break and having fun with my friends. I jog three miles two or three times a week with a male friend. I'm also in a long-distance relationship."

I've given him something. I don't know what *Diagnostic and Statistical Manual of Mental Disorders* label he gives me, and I don't ask.

"These pills should help," he says, and then I'm dismissed.

Why do I need a pill? If I argue, he'll probably request an additional medication.

I have breakfast and lunch with medication for dessert. When the pill's effects kick in, I'm high like I've had one too many drinks. It isn't like the nice energetic buzz that comes with drinking coffee at breakfast.

The psychologists know more about the patients here than the psychiatrist. They are friendly, caring, and upbeat, vastly different from the shrink I saw earlier. So, I decide to wander down the hall to their station, which is surrounded by windows like the first enclosed command center at the entrance.

Everyone looks up when they hear my boots clomping. I give them a big smile and ask, "May I go home today?"

This is when the pill really hits me. I feel my eyes rolling back in their sockets like they're glitching. "I'm trying to see all of you, but I can't control my eyes," I say.

"See that?" It may be the nurse's voice.

"No, I can't," I answer, and they all laugh.

"It looks like she has a vertical nystagmus going on," says the woman who might be a nurse or a psychologist, but I can't read her badge.

"I feel pretty high right now," I say, determined to get out of here. I'm not letting this eye rolling stop me from talking to them about going home.

Through my rapid blinking, I see a tall male open the command center door. He stands right in front of me grinning like this looks very funny.

Cocking my head to one side to see him better makes me look ridiculous. "I'm trying to keep my eyes from fluttering like I'm flirting, but they just won't stop," I tease him.

Everyone laughs again. "It's a side effect of your medication. We need the doctor to order another med to stop your eye rolling. Just hang out here with us. It won't take long," the tall man says.

When I find out phone calls can be made here, I immediately contact Leila to see if she can bring some clothes, toiletries, and my purse. She tells me that she'll come after work with Portia. In the same rush hour traffic, their drive will take three hours.

The psychiatrist orders a second medication, which I get right away. I take it, and eventually my eyes stop rolling around. The pills that I took aren't a solution. My feeling is that I function better without either one. *What are these medications actually doing?*

The grogginess is awful, so I head back to my room and pace to keep from falling asleep. A jog would cure that, but I'm not wearing the right shoes.

Coffee. There is coffee in the rec room. I don't want to show up in the same clothes as yesterday. *Who cares?* I think. *At least I'm not doing the infamous overmedicated shuffle.* I saunter down the hall to the rec room.

Men are sprawled on couches or chairs. Some watch the movie while others read or just stare off. The attitude of the group is bland but not unfriendly. There's just not much chatter or interaction. I make some small talk here and there after grabbing a cup of coffee.

A few men are vacant behind the eyes. Hair is askew and some need a shave—otherwise none of them are badly put together. *Are they just too medicated? Or is this the aftershock from shock therapy, which can affect the memory?*

It's not hard to get small scoops of information. Some men have trouble making eye contact. *Maybe they aren't used to talking to the opposite sex.* When I see scars on wrists, I don't have to ask. No one claims to be someone famous. Most are semi-coherent, but the major thing I notice is a lack of humor.

There are no smiles, eye twinkles, or hints of enthusiasm coming from any of them. It's as though the pizzazz parts of their personalities are just gone. A lackluster grayness rules most of them. *Maybe these men are sedated into their stupefied robotic condition.* Strangely, the psychiatrist isn't too far removed from this same sad state.

Get me out of here. Eight o'clock can't come fast enough. Neither can the next day. Leila arrives in her work clothes with Portia.

We're the only people in the hall as we walk to my room. Leila hands over my weekend bag.

"Thanks for driving all the way here to bring it. It'll feel good to put on some clean clothes," I tell her. "Speaking of driving, I didn't expect to see you behind the unmarked patrol car yesterday."

Leila gives a startled blink. She glances over at Portia and then back at me. "I told Jim you hated cops. But seeing how you two were getting along, I bet he thought I'd been lying about you." She's embarrassed.

"Jim's a caring person and homesick. He's from the East Coast too, so we yakked about the differences between the coasts the whole time," I say.

Portia leans closer to stare at me. I inwardly smile, thinking that I probably look like a nest of disarray without a hairbrush. She gets right to it and out with her judgment. "You don't look unkempt or crazy."

Her remark makes me burst out laughing. "You should have seen me earlier. The pill prescribed caused my eyes to roll like this." I demonstrate it, saying, "So, I needed an additional pill to stop it. These meds don't do a single thing except make me feel like going to sleep. I would get better results from a little tequila."

"Do you know when you're getting out?" Leila sounds more comfortable after my lighthearted response to Portia's comment.

"Maybe tomorrow. The staff will call first and then I'll call you," I say.

"You're ready to leave, right?" Portia stares like she's still searching for some signs of bats in the belfry.

"Oh yes. More than ready, especially after interacting with some of the other patients—all men. There's a big difference between us. If they speak—and they don't say much—there's no sparkle, no interest, and no emotion."

"Why is that?" A look of anguish comes over Leila's face, like she might not be able to handle what I'm about to say.

"I'm not sure, but it's disturbing. It could be surgery, electric shock, or just too many pills. Maybe they'll never get better. Some act this way," I say, imitating a few of them.

Both Leila and Portia look alarmed. "That's scary. We're getting you out of here," says Portia. She's ready to go, and I can't blame her.

Leila lowers her head like she's feeling guilty about calling the authorities. "I'm sorry," she tells me.

"Don't worry. It's not like I'm stuck here forever. Well, you've had a long day and now there's a long drive back. Let's get out of here."

The way Leila, Portia, and I spring up from the bed at the same time gives us the giggles. Other than the staff down the hall, we're the only ones laughing here. "If I ever stop laughing, start shoveling," I say when they hug me.

Later, I wake up with a jolt and think, *Finally*. It's dark when I shower and dress in clean clothes. No staff, no patients, and no counselors are in the rec room when I make a pot of coffee and complete every mundane task written on the blackboard because I'm getting out of here today.

I'm released. Leila and Portia pick me up, and we drive back as though I've never been to a mental institution. We banter like usual and make a stop for some Chinese takeout before we get to the townhouse. We're just sitting down at the table and opening containers when the phone rings. "I'll get it," says Leila, hopping out of her chair.

Even though Leila's in the living room, Portia and I hear her say, "Hello?" She comes back. "It's your sister Helen."

I hand her the chopsticks I've dug from the bag. "Go ahead. Start without me," I whisper, ducking into the living room.

"Hi, Helen. I guess you heard." I tell her about my adventures at the mental institution. "That's the easy part." I take a big breath before telling her about my weird night.

"This is why I'm calling," Helen says after hearing my story. She's silent until she drops a bomb, whispering, "The same thing happened to me."

I'm astonished. "This is the best news I've ever gotten in my life!" I exclaim. "I want to know everything. So, you smelled her then?"

"Yes, just like in Dad's car," Helen whispers.

"Did you get any info that you wrote down? I did, by the way."

"Yes. I wrote things down too."

"Did you feel anything like a big wind or force around you?" I save this question for last because she may have perceived things differently.

"Yes. Whatever was there was huge, and it wouldn't leave. I started drinking tequila hoping to make it go away, but that didn't help at all. It was the scariest thing I've been through. Mother was there—how is that possible?"

"We must be able to go anywhere once we're out of a body. She came to help," I reassure her.

When I ask Helen to tell me more about her experience, she clams up. "I'm afraid that if I talk, it'll hear me and come back," she says.

"Has it come back?"

"No. But it scares me to even think about it. That's it. I don't want to talk about it anymore."

I don't bother pushing Helen to say anything else. I know my sister. It will not help.

Making my voice as soft and soothing as I can to calm her down, I slowly say, "It's okay. I understand how you feel. It's a challenge to even describe it. I wasn't sure I was going to live through it, and Mother protected me. That's why she was there for you too. We don't have to talk about it. Maybe some shots of tequila would have worked better than being taken to a mental institution for a sanity check," I joke. "Seriously, I want you to know that I'm not crazy and neither are you."

"I know we're not. I feel better knowing it didn't only happen to me. I'm sorry, but I just can't talk about it. Thanks for understanding. I love you, sister."

"Don't worry. It's over," I tell her. "It won't come back."

I'm the positive and sunny sister, but I've learned so much from Helen's more negative outlook. The least I can do is help lift her up when she needs it.

"No one else in our family had this experience as far as I know," I say. "They won't have any idea what we're talking about if we ever mention it. Call me anytime. I love you too."

Of course, Leila and Portia have been listening. I pretend I don't know it and sit down to eat. They're probably worried about me, but first things first. It's real food. I can't wait to tell them, but I'm eating some of this food before I do.

There is no way to prepare Leila or Portia for the news, but I have to tell them. "Guess what? You're not going to believe it. The thing that visited me came to visit my sister too. Our mother visited both of us."

Leila looks startled. For once, Portia doesn't seem to know how to respond.

I help by saying, "Helen never wants to talk about it again. She drank tequila until the force or whatever it's called left her house along with our mother. I told her not to worry because it won't come back. Although we live two hundred miles away, our mother visited both of us so we'd know this experience was real and not just in our minds."

Leilah and Portia are still staring like they don't know what to think, but I can't wait. "I'm just going to make a quick phone call," I say.

I call Jeremy to let him know about my sister. Before we hang up, he has one more thing to tell me. "The flies are everywhere." I may be idealistic, but I'm wise enough to know what he means.

8

RUNNER'S HIGH

As Jeremy and I jog along a path, the rhythm of my feet frees my thinking. The atmosphere here is never the same, and it creates ethereal changes while trunks and vine-tangled trees anchor a more permanent reality. Thick, shady foliage all along this trail looks beautifully wearable, smells invitingly scented, and may even be edible.

Seeing the green of dandelion leaves makes me salivate. *I've never met a vegetable I didn't like. Okay. I admit these woods are making me hungry.*

I call out to Jeremy, who jogs behind me. "It's even different today. The temperature here is nothing like the hot-shower stickiness of East Coast humidity. I'm not even sweating much."

Jeremy lets me go ahead after the first mile. Running is more fun when I stay even with him, but my years of playing basketball must give me extra stamina. Sometimes, my daydreams cause me to lose track of the distance between us, which can turn into a quarter mile or more.

"There are lots of microclimates just around here. That's why this trail is never monotonous." From the sound of his voice, I hear Jeremy catching up.

He's wearing running shoes, shorts, socks, and a T-shirt. I've always worn jeans when jogging with him, and today I'm wearing the new pair of jogging socks he gave me.

I notice beads of perspiration on his neck and forehead. His brown hair glistens, but his shirt is still dry. Jeremy has an intense gaze, and at five foot nine inches, he's close to being eye to eye with me. He checks the color of my face, which is probably red by now, and then he looks down at my heavyweight blue jeans. "You'll feel cooler in a pair of jogging shorts," he says.

I give him a contorted grin to make him smile. "So far, I'm okay wearing jeans. My feet feel very comfortable."

Midday during the workweek is a great time for a run. Rarely are other people seen jogging through the beautiful Rancho San Antonio trails. There's no need to worry about time when running with Jeremy. He is a valuable person with an office in a private part of the tech building. No one tells him when to come and go.

I'm still getting used to the West Coast and its weather patterns. Jogging is new for me too. Jeremy has been doing it for years and enjoys that feeling of skimming the ground. Jogging while raining? No problem. Running through mists and light fog is even more of an adventure.

How Do I Know?

The repetitive stepping lulls me into thinking about my new life. I am lucky. My boss hesitated to tackle a computer class and asked me to take her place. I went along with a twenty-four-year-old vice president known as a boy wonder and a young company accountant. I was a new hire and still going to college.

The newly learned computer skills proved to be invaluable. Now I work in the same private office with Jeremy and his assistant, Stella. "He's brilliant and humble," she told me.

I miss my East Coast friends less when the three of us talk. We chat about everything—art, strange adventures of archaeologists in the jungles of the Americas, and even weirder stuff like the paranormal. Jeremy told us about a woman who has an amazing talent. She can locate anyone in the world with a pendulum.

Stella and I let out a simultaneous, "What? How?"

Jeremy took off his tie and got comfortable. He locked his hands behind his head and leaned back in his swivel chair before beginning. "She just needs a picture of the person and a map of the world. She moves the pendulum over the map, and when it begins to swing in a different direction, she announces the individual's location. My brother was looking for someone and was able to find the person with the help of this lady."

Both Jeremy and Stella are open-minded and feel like old friends. I enjoy having conversations with them. It makes my job of creating spreadsheets and working with boring numbers much easier.

The wind along the trail suddenly gusts and briefly shifts my attention. I flick a stray piece of long blond hair out of my eyes and go back to thinking about Jeremy. He is patient, kind, and anything but dull. He doesn't think he's so smart—he has cousins who are like Einstein. He can describe mundane acts like watering a plant in exciting ways.

But what is it exactly that makes him so different? Although I can understand most people, there is something rare about Jeremy. *What is it?* I know it has nothing to do with his being so good in math either. He's comfortable in every situation, like he's got an old soul, but that doesn't explain it.

My pondering will have to be continued. In the meantime, maybe he can answer what I've been hearing from other joggers. I have yet to feel what they call the ultimate running experience. I wait until I'm matching his pace again before asking, "Jeremy, what's this thing called runner's high?"

"It's unique to the individual." He smiles as though my question brings back memories or amusement.

Unique? It's just like Jeremy to give a mysterious answer. While jogging, I'm surprised by the scent of my mother in the breeze. I know it's not just a memory either. It's a visit, but it's not runner's high. I breathe a hello acknowledging her and keep this information to myself.

The runners I've encountered have experienced runner's high, but no one seems to be able to describe it to me. Even with the miles and miles of running I've done in my life, whatever this high is remains a mystery.

I go back to pondering. Some days, a jog starts from the

townhouse where I live, which is about a mile from our workplace. Jeremy gets there first most of the time. He strips off all his work clothes, creating a pile right in front of me like a child. Then in an instant, he slips into his jogging attire. For a while, six coworkers who were on a fitness quest met at my house to run with us during lunch hour. I jokingly called it "the running of the herd." But just like going off a diet, our coworkers stopped running, with only a few reaching their fitness goals. Most of the time only Jeremy and I jog together now.

Recalling a trip to a Japanese restaurant after a jog in the rain, I chuckle. Famished, I kept eating the pickled ginger, not knowing what it was until the order of miso soup and sushi arrived. Jeremy just quietly observed me munching away on all that ginger. Eventually, I learned why it was served and figured out why the waiter kept replenishing it at the sushi bar.

Surprisingly, we had no body odor. The fresh smell of rain was our essence. Over green tea, Jeremy asked, "Why do we cry at perfection?"

I wondered if he'd asked because it made him cry. "I don't know, but I'll search for the answer to such a serious question," I said.

I'm happy that Jeremy and I still jog together. There's nothing more monotonous than sprinting through the sameness of the houses, sidewalks, and streets of the suburbs, so we say bye-bye to that and hello to the woods.

When Jeremy and I reach our favorite part of the trail, we see four reclining limbs of two trees embracing. They appear to be hugging each other while pulling up a sheet of vines for privacy.

"Ha ha ha. Nature has a sense of humor," I yell to Jeremy.

He laughs in agreement. "It wasn't there last time."

After more chuckling and talk of a higher sense of humor, we continue along the path. Our heads are bobbing up and down like a couple of horses.

There is no need to rush. I decide not to run ahead of Jeremy today. He's older, but he's fit with a nice lean build. Jeremy, his wife, and their two children are a happy family and enjoy each other's company. That's also a plus for his health.

Even so, when observing him, I'm reminded of my own mother. My parents had a thirteen-year age difference. My father was older but always healthier, and he still is healthy. Yet my mother was careful about him "overdoing it," as she put it.

As I check Jeremy's color, perspiration, breathing, posture, gait, and yes, even his choice of jogging outfit, all is okay. Just as I'm shifting my gaze away from him, things turn impossible.

I see the familiar old jogging shoes and shorts—that part is normal. At the sight of what isn't normal, my eyes widen and my mouth drops open.

This is it. Runner's high.

Suddenly Jeremy screams, "My God, you just disappeared!"

If Jeremy hadn't blurted that out, I would've assumed what I experienced was runner's high. What I saw would have sounded too crazy to mention. Along with other secrets, I would've kept it to myself.

But Jeremy saw something happen to me at that exact moment. Trying to find out what he thinks, I ask, "Are you the wisest man in the world?" He shakes his head.

I think about what happened. For an instant, Jeremy had looked spliced—like mismatched images on the front of a slot machine turned sideways. From the waist up, he was replaced by the perfect profile of a porpoise. The rest of his body kept running along as usual.

It's hard to believe that he was part porpoise for a few seconds and then went back to normal. *How is it possible?* Of course, my mind is spinning for logic. I'm certain that Jeremy has no easy category for his unique experience either.

"Did you feel anything different when I disappeared?" I had to find out.

"Not a thing. You just vanished right before my eyes." Jeremy sounds elated—even happy.

I don't want to say it, but I can't hold back. "I didn't feel anything either, but I saw you as a porpoise from the waist up, and the other half was you running from the waist down. It wasn't runner's high."

"I believe you. It wasn't runner's high." Jeremy takes this mind-boggling event in stride.

"Well, we're still humans running on planet earth." I'm grateful and admire him for rolling with what just happened.

"We haven't missed a beat," says Jeremy, whose solid nature reassures me.

Neither of us feels as though something crept up on us. We know that much. Both of us are quiet afterward. We are obviously thinking on it.

My mind begins to work like a Magic 8 Ball. *Simultaneous runner's high? No. Hallucination? No. Logical? Try again later.*

I understand what is different about Jeremy. The answer to my question is an odd answer, but it fits. It's just like Jeremy—curious. He must have spent a lifetime as a porpoise. That is what's so unfathomable about him.

It isn't the only thing to become apparent. I realize that I receive answers when tossing questions to the sky, just like throwing a ball that comes back down. Today, that ball came back with an answer about Jeremy. *Thank you.*

Something must have known I'd figure it out. Otherwise, this weird experience wouldn't have been thrown my way.

What we saw was reality. Time and space shifted. To Jeremy, I suddenly disappeared because I wasn't in that lifetime or in the same time frame with him as a porpoise. The view of him from the waist down was a reference point, and it was visible because I *was* in the running time frame with him.

"I bet you know every pattern there is," Jeremy concludes—like a cryptic statement coming out of the blue.

How Do I Know?

At the end of our run, I'm leaning against the car, still wearing jeans, and cooling off. Jeremy puts on his regular clothes and comes over to me. With his most serious, penetrating look, he simply says, "We just accept some things."

9

THE PHYSICS LESSON

The sounds echo all the way to the depths of the underground, breaking into my sleep like waves of water going through me. I rise back up to some awareness of the room. At the crossroads, I could choose to ignore it and drift back down, but curiosity takes over.

Surfacing to alertness, I find myself on my back just the way I went to bed. My sleepy eyes don't want to, but they're opening and adjusting to the dark.

Is that you? I reach for the six-foot-two-inch lump under the covers that is my boyfriend, Jared. *Have I finally caught you snoring?* Checking, I feel the gentle rise and fall of his chest. His breathing is slow and soft, so it's obvious he's not the source of what woke me.

I close my eyes knowing he's sleeping peacefully next to me. Our home in a serene woodsy area is quiet at night compared to where we used to live. At our old place, we had to contend with blaring car horns waking us up like clock alarms going off too early.

It's easy to drift back down. I don't even realize I've fallen asleep until I'm startled awake by a thump. Then comes a long scratch and more thumps.

I'm not moving until I figure out what's making that noise. This isn't going to turn into a creature like the one in Lisa's guest room, is it? That was the East Coast. This is the West Coast.

It's quiet until a sound like nails on a chalkboard causes a repelling shiver to go through me. Not being able to pinpoint the source is unsettling.

A streetlight shining on a hill next to our house illuminates the bedroom curtains. My night vision is good. In the semidarkness I can locate the top of a small wooden table across from the bed, but there's not enough light to see the carved designs along its front apron.

When the sounds start up again, I track them along the wide doorway. Something hits the open shoji screen door in the front right corner of the bedroom and my heart jumps. I don't dare move in case I need to play dead.

A shadowy shape jumps up and down. It's Spock, our feral black cat, who usually stays outside at night. Jared and I gave him an alien's name because humans didn't raise him.

Oh, that's all it is. Blowing a big breath of relief out through my mouth like a trumpet player, I laugh at myself for being startled by nothing.

Spock jumps and swats at the wall again, going berserk. When he keeps this up, I glance over at my man, who hasn't moved. *How can it be?* He's still sound asleep.

Okay. It looks like I'm going to have to get out of bed and help Spock. It wouldn't be the first time I've hunted with a cat. I make myself a large menace while the cat stalks low bushes and smaller spaces. We work as a unit until we either get the prize or we drive the intruder out of our territory.

What's in our territory now? Just as I'm about to get up to find out, Spock stops. He's like a black stone doorstop standing guard in the dim light. *Good. Finally.*

But there's some movement in a small area of the wall about six feet up. Spock sees it too and must be fascinated because he's still frozen. I wait for him to get it before springing out of bed to help.

Something oozes right where Spock's been pouncing. My one leg already out of the bed freezes. At the sight of a light gray blob, I gasp. My mind tries to name it. *Ectoplasm? There's no medium here. What's the source of it?*

The ooze is growing larger on the wall, and it's only feet away from the end of my side of the bed. A low-relief profile of a face emerges. It forms into a real head. I can't look away.

I try lassoing thoughts to slow my fight-or-flight response. One foot is still on the floor. I swing that leg back onto the bed and grab for the comforter, pulling it up to disguise myself. My back is against the wall.

More of a man's body is coming out, illuminated by the light outside. He's real. I can't move—he's too close. Jared's right next to me, but I'm too enthralled and frozen in place to wake him.

Fresh from the wall, the man continues walking in a straight line and passes the foot of our bed. He is a life-size Native American in full headdress.

This is it. My body shakes. *No, wait—he isn't turning and reaching for me like a story monster.* My mouth springs open in surprise. *No? He's not a ghost? Well, what is he then?*

My eyes are glued to a real man directly across from me who is still looking ahead. His eyes aren't focused on me, and he doesn't turn to look in my direction. It's like he's oblivious to my presence. He strides across the bedroom, heading straight to the opposite wall. He walks right through it like the house isn't here, and then he's gone.

Of course, my mind buzzes for a while. *Would have, could have*—it happened so fast. I wonder why I didn't think to wake the only other human witness. *Jared's never seen a spirit. He would have loved it.* No special eyes were needed. Anyone with normal eyesight would have experienced it. I wonder if it was coincidence that Spock was attacking the wall. If he hadn't been, I would've slept right through it. *Did he wake me up to see this? That's far-fetched—why would he?* He did sense something before the man was visible, though.

I find no physical evidence of the man. Miwok people lived in the area near the creek, and they pushed their canoes off from this low point near the San Francisco Bay. Only their chieftains wore headdresses. If I could turn back the spiraling clock of time, I might be in the chief's flesh-and-blood present—now the past from my perspective. *That's it. He's in his lifetime, but he looked like a hologram from where I am—inside my body in atomic-clock time.*

I know he won't come back to haunt me, but he could walk through my bedroom again—it's on the ground floor. I wonder if my gentle cat, who keeps his claws tucked in when we play, will give me another heads-up.

Our bodies live in biological time. The chief has long since dropped his body, but what's left is like a recording—a movie of him living in that time frame.

Who will he, you, or I become in the future if our energy—soul— once created can't be destroyed?

What a physics lesson. Nothing is lost. Nothing gets away. If the physics of the planet recorded the chief, it's recording us.

Past, present, future—it's not the end now, is it?

10

THE LIGHT YEAR

My peripheral vision captured something as I stepped behind my office door to hang my coat. When I swung the door back open, I saw Keith slapping at the air in his office across the hall. To keep from laughing at his dance moves, I had to turn around.

I checked my phone for messages with a big smile on my face and then glanced up to sneak a peek at him. We locked eyes. Keith held my attention by touching his ear and beckoning me closer with his other hand.

Putting both hands on my hips, I asked, "Are you swatting at me?" I tried to appear riled up as I walked into his office and sat down.

Keith flashed a peace sign and started right in. "You have to go see her. Judy told me last week I'd get the job and the department would be relocating. She said my girlfriend wasn't the one. How could she know when I hadn't told her anything?"

Keith was my boss. He'd received his MBA two years earlier and had been working at this tech company ever since. Down to earth and practical, he was the last sort of person you'd think would recommend a psychic to someone.

I'd never seen Keith this animated. Human resources for the tech giant *did* call. He'd gotten the job and yes, the department was moving soon. His family was so close that his girlfriend would be marrying them too. He loved her, but she didn't click with his mom, and that was a big problem. Keith had been conflicted for some time. His girlfriend could be the right one, and that's the reason why he'd sought the help of a seer named Judy.

This action of Keith's came as a surprise, but I understood. Sometimes, the normal route doesn't help with a solution.

I gave him support. "You saw the right person for advice. I'm blown away by the accuracy of her predictions. She's impressive."

"See? You should go see Judy," said Keith, pushing thick black bangs aside with his pen. It wasn't uncommon for him to challenge me or egg me on to follow his lead.

"Okay, give me the number." I sighed. If Keith detected something in my voice, he didn't say anything. The sadness over my mother's passing could still come at any time and stay for an instant—or longer.

He nodded approvingly before saying, "You won't regret it. I've seen her twice. She's able to pick up right where she left off from my first visit. Here's another thing—it's good to take a shower before you see her."

"Why is that?"

Keith shrugged and adjusted his tie. "I don't understand it myself, but some psychics can smell a person. And get this—smell them even before they arrive for the appointment."

This info was new to me, and I wondered what Judy had told him. Keith never had bad breath or body odor.

"Judy doesn't even need you to be there. She can find you by age, hair color, and location. And she sometimes follows up with clients after their visit—just to see how they're doing."

"I'll think about making an appointment." I didn't feel an urge to see a psychic, but I decided to keep Judy's number just in case.

His phone rang. "I have to take this call. Go for a reading. I'd like to hear what she says about you."

"By the way, congratulations," I whispered, sticking my thumb to my nose and waving my fingers like I was opening a fan. I walked back to my office.

O

Keith had me thinking about my first-ever visit to a psychic named Moriah. It was when I was at my old workplace. I was skeptical. Asking around at work meant sticking my neck out, but I did it anyway.

When I asked if anybody knew a good psychic, I didn't expect the rapid response from my coworkers. They unanimously agreed on a female tech-marketing person who could help me. Straightaway, I walked to her office. Then I hesitated and stood outside her doorway.

Curiosity prevailing, I introduced myself and let the marketer know who'd referred me before voicing my request. "I've never been to a psychic," I confessed. The conservatively dressed woman didn't have to think even for a moment. Without any delay, she scribbled a phone number she knew by heart and the name Moriah.

"Moriah has helped me many times. She's honest and her predictions are accurate." The marketer also revealed personal information that was generally not forthcoming in the corporate world, where people take care to protect their image. My perspective shifted as I discerned that she wasn't the regular corporate type.

On the day of the reading, my reliable Volkswagen wouldn't start. Even though a car is just an inanimate object, it felt as though I'd been let down personally. I gave the car a damning look, and for anyone in or out of a body to hear, I added, "I don't care if you don't start. I will see this psychic even if I have to walk." I would see Moriah. I had my reasons, and nothing would prevent me from going. I had to find out if my mother was okay and discover if psychics were real.

How Do I Know?

My girlfriend Portia dropped me off in front of a charming house with a trellis and birdbath in the yard. Bird feeders with perches dangled from trees and poles. Flowers bloomed around the yard, and a statue of a woman with a bird at her feet stood on the porch near the front door.

Moriah greeted me with sharp hazel eyes and a gentle welcome as we introduced ourselves. We sat in her living room, where the afternoon sun streamed through two beautiful floor-to-ceiling windows. It bounced from mirrors to glass objects, creating sparkles on shelves and bright streaks across the marble fireplace mantel.

I settled into a comfortable chair. Moriah sat in the other armchair. A teapot, a pitcher of water, and cups on a pewter tray were on the small table between us.

Nothing was gloomy or creepy about the room, which put me more at ease. There were no crystal balls, fortune cards, or smoky concoctions anywhere. She didn't have any stereotypical seer fanfare shown in movies.

The reading started like an interview because I asked so many questions. I wanted a crash course in Psychics 101.

Moriah indulged me, explaining how she saw a major war before it started. She'd asked her mother why eggs were dropping from airplanes in the sky. Moriah didn't know about bombs, and eggs were what they looked like to her three-year-old mind. She told me about her abilities and how she received information. She also worked with spirits and mischievous poltergeists.

When I asked Moriah about the afterlife, she shared personal knowledge of it. She also gave reassurances that my mother was just fine. There wasn't even a hint of sadness when she spoke. Her description of my mother was accurate, and that helped me accept more of her information.

Two hours into the reading, Moriah repositioned herself. She casually put an elbow on the table and cupped her chin with a hand holding a few strands of silvery hair. With a relaxed stare, as if she was taking a long look at me for the first time, she said, "Ask me what you came here to ask."

Moriah waited, giving me more than enough time, but no question came to me. What was wrong with me? It was rare for my mind to be one big blank, but I couldn't think of anything to ask for myself.

Moriah broke the silence. "Why am I seeing so much light around you?"

I didn't know what Moriah meant, but ideas popped into my mind right away, as they usually do. "Oh. Maybe it's because I paint, and my paintings are colorful. I use a computer for six to eight hours a day, so its light could be what you're seeing." I offered this information and waited for her to verify it.

Moriah's response was just a look. In fact, she said nothing at all about my answers. She didn't ask me anything more, but she did wear a hint of a smile. It was the kind of smile a grown-up has when the subject is too adult for a child.

Neither of us said anything for a few minutes. *So, this must be it—the end.*

I almost missed the little Donation Only sign on a pedestal near the doorway. Just as the marketing person had said, payment could be anything or nothing at all.

"Thank you for the reading, Moriah. It's obvious you love what you do."

I respectfully placed my money in an ornate offering plate on an altar. Although I had extra cash for transportation home, I'd come up with a plan. If Moriah gave me a ride, I would give it to her.

"Blessings and many thanks to you, Diana. It's rare for a visitor to ask about me. I enjoyed telling you about my life. My psychic abilities have allowed me to help so many. I believe in using these gifts for the good and in service to others. Now, just how are you planning on getting home?" Apparently, Moriah noticed a car delivering me to her house.

"By cab. My car wouldn't start this afternoon."

"I'll give you a ride," Moriah insisted. "Oh, where are my keys? The car keys were right here. Those poltergeists must have hidden them."

I wanted to burst out laughing. *Hmm. Poltergeists? Maybe just misplaced?* I helped Moriah with the search.

"An evening drive will charge the battery. Okay. I found them." Moriah twirled the keys and gave a salute with them in hand. For her, it was a victory over the poltergeists.

It was a fast trip home because Moriah didn't drive like an elderly person. I slipped her the money and we talked for a few more minutes before she drove off. I hadn't expected to get clarity and a lighter heart when it came to my mother's passing, but I did.

O

A few months after giving me Judy's number, Keith left the company to start his new job, and he called to give me an update. "The department is relocating now. I broke up with my girlfriend and I'm seeing someone new. She impresses my family, and she gets along with Mom," he said. Everything had come true for Keith just as Judy predicted. I told him I hadn't called Judy yet but that I'd quit my job at our old tech company.

Keith's call got me thinking about my relationship. Jared and I had spent ages keeping in touch with phone calls and handwritten letters. I'd slept with a photograph of him that I put on the pillow next to me. Sometimes, I'd wake up to find it stuck to my neck or face.

Jared laughed when I told him about it. It made me sad when areas of the photograph started to crack and then crumble and fall apart like he was disappearing from my life. As a remedy, I drew parts of his face back in with a black pen and white liquid corrector. My handiwork didn't look bad either. Finally, after nine months, I was able to throw it away when the actual Jared moved to the West Coast to be with me.

How Do I Know?

On the night of Keith's call, it was the third full moon of the year. There was a chill in the air. I looked up from my book and imagined Jared racing from the bus stop about now, raising his body temperature, beating the cold, and heading home. This man didn't just walk, he strode.

When the front door opened, he found me curled up on the sofa with our two black cats. The three of us sprang up to meet him. We had a greeting ritual—kisses, hugs, and petting our cats.

"It might be too chilly to go for a walk after dinner tonight. It'll make me walk faster, but you can always keep up with me," he said.

"I'll use you as a shield and hang on to your arm. That'll keep me warmer, plus it'll slow you down so I don't rip the kick pleat of another vintage skirt."

"Sorry about that. You tucked around me feels good. So, go ahead, slow me down."

Jared was an intelligent and serious man who could deliver one icy-looking stare, but that never fazed me. I thought he secretly liked me to poke him every now and then to loosen him up. His handsome features, quiet poise, and height, along with his piercing gray eyes, could intimidate the hell out of people. They didn't realize he was sensitive too.

We had a young love and a new life beginning for both of us. As Jared and I relaxed in each other's arms and chatted about our upcoming trip to Newport Beach, we dozed off.

When our eyes opened at the same time, I got silly. "Oh, we get to make a wish. We spoke with our eyes at the same time, didn't we? That counts. That's a match, so let's make a wish."

Being silly rubbed off and Jared started tickling me. He showed some mercy and stopped when he had me shrieking. I caught my breath and we both calmed down.

"Is this where we hook our pinky fingers together before we start wishing?" he asked.

Maybe Mr. Serious hasn't played this game? I gave a wink and a nod.

"Okay. Let's do it. Hmm, bet you can't guess mine," he murmured.

We hooked our pinkies together, closed our eyes, and started wishing. I knew I was taking too long when his finger started to wiggle. "Wait. If you let go, it won't come true," I said.

He waited until I opened my eyes. Then, without a word, he pulled me closer, taking me in his arms, pressing his assured lips on mine. As he whispered love affirmations, I touched the corners of his sweet mouth.

When he kissed me again, an electrical spark went from my mouth down to my toes. I wondered if he felt it, and then I felt him smile. My heart surged with a warm, happy feeling, and I let out a long murmur of delight.

How Do I Know?

We didn't stop, and I slid my fingers down his side, stroking him. He drew in a quick breath, pressing me to feel his reaction. I held on to him as my head fell back.

Jared's voice was passionate. "I love kissing you," he said, cradling my head while caressing my shoulders and back.

A secret message came into my mind—a thought I'd had for a long time. *I don't want my love to lose his way.* This was why I wore the same cologne—so he could always find me. It was strange to think of it right then.

Jared shifted to massage me and I swayed into him, letting out eager little breaths. "I love it," I whispered, reaching to caress him back.

The moon created an alluring glimmer shining through the window, making our skin look otherworldly with an irresistible blue glow. We were two lovers, very close—nice and tight in the sensual moonlight.

We stared into each other's eyes. When his hands moved lower, my back arched. "Your blue skin is bewitching," he said enthusiastically. Then he said softly, "Let's slow down for a second."

"Mm. I'm over the moon in love with you," I said, relaxing with him.

Jared snuggled my ear, then gently tugged my earlobe. "I love you too," he whispered, running his fingers through my hair.

The full moon thrilled like good mood music. As we paused under the spell of its magical beams, I thought to be in love when making love—nothing else is above that.

We were illuminated and seduced by this enchanting moonlight as we fit together. Jared rocked me into a new pleasurable plateau, causing me to go into a trance. My eyes closed as my thoughts drifted away with his motions. He created waves of sensual love vibrations, and I was a floating receptive vessel.

In this dreamy state, a mysterious presence spontaneously entered my mind, causing a kind of coitus interruptus. I felt intense joy from its enrapturing light. Its stunning form was an extraordinary visual experience, giving me the most love I had ever felt and the most beauty I'd ever seen.

What I witnessed had four concentric oval rings of light flowing like water. The form's oval center was the smallest in size, and it radiated a beautiful violet color. Surrounding it was a radiating cobalt-blue oval light encircled by an even larger oval ring vibrating a brilliant sun-colored yellow. The surrounding outermost oval glowed a splendorous snow white and reached to the edges of my mind as it danced alongside thin darker lines waving in between its brilliance. The rippling darker lines were like rays moving within each of the four oval rings.

The structure remained stationary in my mind's eye, yet its rays moved gracefully in their positions. The brightness filled my mind like a shining jewel.

How Do I Know?

I didn't hear its approach, it didn't crackle or spit like fire, and it didn't make a sound when it left. I wanted to know why it showed up in the middle of our lovemaking, what it was, who it was, and what it meant.

After it vanished, I kept rerunning its beautiful reality because I wanted it with me always and I couldn't stop thinking about it.

I felt as though I'd been somewhere else. My enchanted mind returned to Jared, who hadn't stopped moving. His breathing guided me back like an aphrodisiac. In the sensual aura of erotic blue moonlight, I caught up to him.

We held each other in a blue afterglow before leisurely untangling our limbs. My hand moved gently to his heart, then I held his beautiful face in my hands and waited for him to tell me if something unusual had happened. I wanted him to describe it first. Although the visitor's presence came to my mind and body, he could have experienced it too. I figured maybe he'd be worried about what I might think.

As I waited, my private sense of humor kicked in. *I can assure Jared that whatever he's heard about the proverbial light coming on— what I saw might not be it. See the light? Saw the light? What does that even mean—what kind of light? Ha. It's not my first orgasm. Since I'm more of a practical girl—pregnant?*

I decided to set the tone before talking about the extraordinary phenomenon. "That was an *extra* good wish," I murmured. "Did anything happen to you?" I looked at him with half-closed eyes and a playful smile.

He chuckled. "What do you mean, Diana?" Jared's voice was calm and reassuring. He was never easily rattled.

A memory of my mother reminded me to slow down when speaking. I took my time, saying, "Something like a radiating flame appeared in my mind. It was like being visited."

Jared was quiet, so I continued. "It radiated intense love and joy. How is that possible? I've never seen or felt anything so beautiful. I could have died happily after that."

"Nothing like that happened to me," he confirmed. Well at least he wasn't telling me that it didn't occur.

"It's not my imagination. Maybe it's documented someplace, and if not—I'll draw it. I can't be the only one to have this experience. The love it gave is like our lovemaking."

Jared smiled. "Show me your drawing and let me know what you find out."

His words reassured me. "Oh. What if it means I'm pregnant? If I take birth control pills, I'm slow like a slug." *Jared wasn't wearing a condom.*

"We'll just have to wait and see." This was Jared's unflappable response.

That's easy for you to say. I didn't voice this thought.

How Do I Know?

The seer Moriah asked why she saw so much light around me. Maybe she knew this was going to happen when I was having sex, so that's why she gave me the grown-up kind of look. Remembering her expression, I grinned.

I thought of Judy, the psychic Keith had urged me to visit. I hadn't seen her yet because I didn't have any reason to go. I wasn't looking for love—well, maybe looking for a new job, but I knew I'd get one soon enough.

"Good night, love," Jared said as he set the alarm clock and yawned.

"Sweet dreams. I love you."

"You know I love you too."

Once we were quiet and still, I felt a light pounce and then another one. It was just our cats settling at the foot of our bed like a pair of foot warmers.

It felt like the time was right to contact Judy.

11

THE DAY VISITATION

The cup of black coffee I drink makes me edgy, so I try some tricks to relax, like clenching my toes and fingers and then letting them go limp. It isn't just the coffee making me nervous—my own mind is doing it. My stomach feels queasy because it's the day of the reading with Judy. A shower and shampoo help to put the dizzy thoughts in my head to sleep.

For comfort, I put on black jeans and a T-shirt and reach for the distinctive bottle of Chanel No. 5 just to inhale its aroma. It works to transport me to an imaginary sanctuary filled with flowers and greenery. I catch the scent of freesias because these are in bloom all over the hillside across the street and must get mixed into the whiff.

It's a two-hour drive to Judy's home. I rush up seven stone steps to our street-level garage, excited about this new adventure. As I jump into my sports car and adjust the sunroof, a few unexpected jitters overtake me again. I glance at the clock—it's time to leave and head toward the ocean.

How Do I Know?

Driving this route is a way to experience a vacation-like effect thanks to the two beautiful views—the San Francisco Bay on the left and the Pacific Ocean to the right—when crossing the Golden Gate Bridge. The colorful houses along Nineteenth Avenue in the city of San Francisco wouldn't have been acceptable in the muted wood-and-earth neighborhood where I grew up. Their uniqueness is a treat.

Driving on scenic Interstate 280 in light traffic is too much temptation, so I race along the empty lanes at seventy-five to eighty-five miles per hour or faster. Flying down the highway like a ball of fire, I make great time.

I knock at Judy's front door, and a natural-looking woman with intense blue eyes and long, wavy brown hair opens it. Smiling as she introduces herself, Judy is much younger than the psychic I saw four years earlier, Moriah.

There's a calmness in Judy's eyes and softness to her steps as we walk down the hall to her reading room. Inside are symbols related to her profession and her soul's choice. Paintings of goddesses and angels, spiritual books, flowers, amethysts, and other unfamiliar semiprecious stones are set on shelves mounted to the wall.

As Judy sits down behind a table, she makes a sweeping gesture for me to choose either chair in front of it. Under the window next to her is a small wooden table. On it is a box of tissues and a recording device. Both look out of place compared to the other decor.

I make myself comfortable in a chair across from her. She makes small talk as she turns on the equipment, telling me that I'll get an audio version of my reading.

She clasps her hands gently, revealing a large amethyst ring in a yellow gold setting. "Okay," she murmurs in the direction of her equipment before looking at me intently. "Ready?"

I nod. *Ready or not, here it comes.*

In mere seconds, Judy places herself in a visibly hypnotic state. Her closed eyes flutter strangely. "Let me begin with the personality. You were born with an extremely sharp mental status," she says. She clears her throat, then continues. "You operate in the function of the goddess and reincarnate during critical periods in the world to channel energy so that certain things can take place for mankind. This is the reason for your incarnating at this time." In her trance state, she says all this without even looking at me.

Hearing these words is like running on sand dunes to experience your first sight of the sea horizon and getting the disorienting-reorienting feeling the ocean's power brings until your eyes settle into the rhythm of the incoming waves, the outgoing water, and you steady yourself to balance its endowments by grounding on the shore.

Judy isn't through, so I just listen. "You lived primarily in Egypt and Greece, where you were a priestess and a healer," she says. "You were trained in the mysteries or the occult, although the latter word has somewhat negative connotations today." She checks in to make sure I'm okay with the word occult.

"It's fine," I say. "I don't equate it only with witchcraft."

Just when I think it can't get any weirder, she continues, telling me what it means to be trained in the mysteries. "In Egypt, you could focus your mind and your will so that objects in the form of visions would appear out of thin air for others to see," she says matter-of-factly.

Judy's reading for Keith left him in awe of her. I'm a real questioner, but the fact that Keith's reading was so accurate could mean that mine—odd as it is—might be true too.

She says, "You have a great deal of love for humankind. You have evolved very far."

Suddenly, I feel so affected by Judy's wisdom that tears just start rolling. "Did you bring these just for me?" I'm embarrassed when Judy hands me a couple of tissues. We have a laugh because so many of her clients cry.

According to her, I've learned my craft well. "By choice, this is your first lifetime outside the temple," she says. She tells me that I was associated with the writer of the book of Revelations. She says I'm closest to the person known as the beloved. "Forgive us for not telling you the name," she continues. Judy's tone is serious, and her words are puzzling. "Forgive" is a strange choice. And I wonder who she means by "us."

"While you have a very loving relationship, you're going to meet a man who has the same awareness as you," she tells me.

It startles me to hear her say that Jared won't be my lifelong mate. I am unaware of my response to this, which is to envelop her like a spider, creating the need for her to protect herself. Although I haven't changed my physical position, she raises her arm, the palm of her hand facing out as if to push me back. Gently, she says, "It's okay, it's okay."

"What's wrong?" I ask her.

Judy lets me know that my spontaneous emotional response felt like something invisible grabbing her. "This is a normal reaction when we hear things we don't want to hear."

"I didn't realize that I was hurting you. I'm sorry," I say, feeling clueless.

Judy reassures me that she's okay and knows I didn't mean to inflict anything uncomfortable on her. She does have this to say about it. "While I can tell you what you want to know, ultimately you will learn to find out for yourself. You wouldn't just accept anyone's words regarding fate and prophecy anyway. You are one who has to make up her own mind about these things."

She remains mysterious about the man who will become my partner, saying, "You will meet your husband, but not in the normal sense."

What? It sounds spooky.

This is when Judy encourages me by saying, "You know you can do it."

"Today, a goddess is reduced to a creature whose only attributes are sex appeal and beauty. I'm glad this isn't what you're talking about." I can't help but mention it.

"Really." Judy nods in agreement. Then she floors me. "I don't know the future any more than you do." On top of that she adds, "You are extremely psychic. Think of us as a peer group."

How Do I Know?

I recall Moriah's psychic talents. Moriah could see everyone's fate but her own. She hadn't mentioned my abilities to see into time. We'd only talked about how it is to be psychic. Now, Judy is telling me that my gifts are like her own. *No way.*

Judy gives me a teacher's formidable look. Her already intense eyes blaze as she strongly emphasizes her words. "Your job is to learn how energy works. You will be much happier once you are able to utilize your powers."

When my reading is over, Judy holds out her arms and gives me a hug along with my recording. This is always her way of ending a session.

I get in my car thinking, *No cookie-cutter reading for me.* I'd get the peculiar one, of course. But Judy's words resonate with me—taking me back to the maple tree's leafy branches, where I hid with my cat to read about goddesses. In this Greek religion, extraordinary goddesses of love, wisdom, and power also watched over and guided human beings.

This is what I am? I try to rally myself by saying if I've been a goddess many times, I can do this again. I won't be an arrogant one who says, "You heard me—kiss my wing."

As I drive, I listen to my reading. Some of it sounds so weird that I replay the parts about temple abilities several times because I don't understand what Judy means.

My mind is reaching all right. *So, now where am I? All the way to Novato?* I drive to the next exit to turn around and head south again on Highway 101.

O

When the traffic slows down for roadwork, I see a male figure standing underneath the arched overpass. We stuck drivers gain mere inches in a ho-hum dance of one-two footwork with our gas pedals, clutches, and brakes. Only the remote man has escaped, being herded into one lane like the rest of us.

It takes a while to get to the overpass with the man underneath, but we've moved just a speck, so I'm close enough to get a better look. It looks like he's rolling a cigarette or something. He holds the roll to his mouth and licks it. Swooping his fingers over his wavy honey-brown hair, he positions the cigarette so that it's perched behind his right ear.

When traffic comes to a stop, I'm shaded beneath the overpass and the man is now a few yards away. He's wearing jeans and a black shirt. There's a backpack on the ground next to him. He looks like a Hells Angel.

There's something different about him. I can't explain it.

It's not because his thumb isn't out for a ride. Even if it was, I don't pick up hitchhikers as a rule. Still, something pushes me to find out more. I react to it by lowering the passenger window.

While the man looks rough on the outside, that doesn't mean he's a messed-up soul. I can't say why I'm going to break my own rule. I'm following an inner prompting when I ask, "Where are you going? Do you need a ride?"

The man looks surprised. Maybe it's my car—midnight blue and celestial—that prompts his expression.

"Yes. To the bridge," he replies.

"Which bridge?" I'm only familiar with two of them, and there are eight in the San Francisco Bay Area.

"The bridge over to the East Bay," he tells me.

"Okay," I say, leaning to reach the front passenger door handle to let him in.

The medium-built man sits down with an agile move. I notice a gold ring on his left hand as he lowers his sunglasses to look directly at me with clear brown eyes. "Thanks," he says, and he puts his backpack on the floor between his boots.

Nosy me—I can't help myself. "Are you a Hells Angel?" Ruff, ruff—it just blurts out. *I'm not judging—only trying to perceive him because I've never met a Hells Angel before.*

"Why, I just took off my jacket about ten minutes ago." He sounds a little taken aback. He thoughtfully rubs the brown stubble on his chin and eyes me curiously.

Right. That's a careful answer. I give a shy smile. "I'm new to the area. You'll have to show me the way."

"Okay," says the Hells Angel. "What's your name?"

Even though he's a Hells Angel, I feel comfortable because I don't think he's lied to me. I tell him my name.

He says, "I'm Jack. My number is three." This is a first—a number and no last name. Jack doesn't elaborate. Three might be his favorite number, but to state a number after giving your name is odd and it strikes me as funny.

"Well, I have a number too," I say. *And it has nothing to do with numerology.* "I'm number thirteen—lucky thirteen, not the unlucky thirteen." I giggle.

Jack unzips his leather backpack and pulls out his wallet. "I live in Sacramento. Can I show you some photos?" When I nod, Jack hands me a photo. "This is my wife."

His wife is also a brunette. She has a confident look and a nice light in her eyes. "She's a good woman," I say.

"You're right about that. Here's our baby boy," he says.

The traffic is starting to move faster. With an eye on the road, I hold up the photo. Jack's son looks happy. His face has that adorable, good-fairy quality. "Oh, those sweet cheeks—what a good little elf."

"Love is everything." Jack smiles.

"I agree," I say, handing the photos back to him.

Love. Maybe I can talk to him about odd things like the mysterious visitor light that shined a certain way. I have the feeling Jack can handle it.

"I just got the weirdest reading from a psychic named Judy. My boss recommended her because he got such an incredibly accurate reading. He kept insisting that I see her, but I didn't have any reason until I had a strange encounter with a beautiful light." I described its colorful radiating concentric rings, its brightness, and the feeling of love and bliss it delivered.

Jack leans forward, so I add, "The psychic said that I operate in the function of the goddess and reincarnate during critical times. A goddess? I'm trying to figure out what this even means."

Jack's mouth opens slightly, and he gives me a look of wonder. "I've been looking all over San Francisco for you!" he exclaims, putting the family photos away and pulling a piece of paper from his backpack.

So, my light experience is why people will come looking for me? Or is it because of what Judy's reading revealed about me? I say nothing, waiting to find out why Jack was looking for me—just in case.

Jack holds a small piece of paper in his right hand. "I'm a poet. I'd like to read you one of my poems."

"I'd love to hear it."

"The title is 'My Goddess,'" he says, and he begins reading in a low, clear voice.

My Goddess wears a necklace of the brightest stars aglow.

My Goddess wears a silver crown and flakes of purest snow.

A. Wolfe

My Goddess wears a field of green and seas of
ocean blue,

My Goddess wears soft golden sands and rays of
sunlight too.

My Goddess wears white silky clouds and
autumn leaves and dreams,

My Goddess wears a robin's song and diamond
sparkling streams.

My Goddess wears the woodland's hush and
beads of falling rain,

My Goddess wears the soul of peace and
laughter's sweet refrain.

My Goddess wears a kitten's joy, a rainbow, and
a rose,

My Goddess wears a baby's cry, and midnight's
velvet clothes.

My Goddess wears a summer day; my Goddess
wears the night,

My Goddess wears a child's touch, a woman's
love, and style.

How Do I Know?

My Goddess wears the hope of man—my
Goddess wears a smile.

"I want you to have this poem," says Jack after reading it.

"I'm honored to receive it. In a single day, I have a beautiful goddess poem from you and a goddess reading from a psychic, although I'm still trying to figure that one out." I sigh.

"You'll figure it out. I know you will," says Jack. He sounds like he means it.

We're near the bridge when I decide *not* to pull over. "I'll take you across the bridge. You won't get a ride here with these cars flying by because there's no good place to stop."

It's a beautiful day this March 11, and the water sparkles as we cross the bridge. I pull into the tollbooth parking lot.

"I didn't plan to drive so far north on Highway 101 today. I was replaying my reading and missed my exit by twenty miles."

Jack's head tips back as he chuckles. "I'm lucky that you did."

"I get lucky when I pull U-turns," I say.

We exit the car at the same time, and I step to the rear to open the trunk. "I'd like to give you something in return for your poem. Your choice."

Jack chooses an art print. "I like this one because it reminds me of today with the bridge, the water, and the city."

"The inspiration came from my mind, but it's this view all right. Oh, wait a minute." I fish through prints. "Okay. This one's yours. See— its number is three."

Jack carefully rolls it like that cigarette still behind his ear and puts it in his backpack. He looks pleased. "Here I was looking all over for you, and you found me. I'll never forget you."

"It took me getting lost to meet you. I'll never forget you or this day either."

I make a U-turn and head back across the bridge. It's been a day for the word *goddess*, which hasn't been tossed around this much since I read Greek mythology in elementary school. What an uncanny set of coincidences.

Jack's words echoed Judy's. "You know you can do it," she'd said.

O

When I finally get home, I curl up with my two black cats and don't leave our blue couch. In the woodsy quiet, my mind replays the way this warm winter day unfolded.

I listen to my reading again, hoping to grasp its strange reality so I can work with the energy Judy talked about. My cats, Astro and Spock, are on either side of me—each has his head on one of my thighs. They stay put—maybe they like the sound of Judy's voice.

It's nearly dark when the door opens and my tall, handsome man with his strong, lithe frame steps inside. He pulls off a blue scarf and removes his jacket.

"Did you see Judy? How'd it go?" he asks.

The cats and I don't jump up as usual. "Come over here and sit with us. Yes, I did. She gave me a recording of the session. I'll warn you—it's not like Keith's reading," I say.

"That's even better. Let's hear it before dinner." When he picks up Spock and snuggles closer to give me a kiss, Astro jumps in my lap and purrs. We're one happy little family.

Jared listens intently to my reading without any of the questioning looks I'd given Judy. His slender musician's fingers massage Spock's head and ears. He's a steady listener with a true musician's ear like my mother's.

He synthesizes my reading after hearing about my abilities and the reason for incarnating. He compares me to King Arthur's court magician, proclaiming, "Wow, just like a Merlin."

Days later, I phone Jared at work to say, "I just got a temporary computer job with late-afternoon hours. It's not like my old white-collar tech job with that long commute—it's local. It could lead to something better. I'll tell you more later."

O

In my new workplace, every employee is into the paranormal. It makes our six-hour shifts more interesting than working with data inside a cubicle. We talk about true dreams, visions, seeing ghosts, psychic predictions, and all kinds of odd things that you don't talk to just anyone about.

Even our boss, Greer, is into things like consciousness and ESP. He reads academic and scientific books on these subjects, which also interests me. He shares the titles and tells me, "These researchers are experimenting with what the mind can do."

This gets my attention in a big way, but I change the subject, saying, "Keep an eye on the ground when you walk because you'll see all kinds of strange things. Years ago, I found an old leather case in the curve of a freeway exit full of debris. It had a camel, a pyramid, palm trees, and engraved initials on it. The middle letter, *J*, was the only difference—otherwise it had the same initials as mine. The case was nice, but I couldn't use it, so I gave it away."

Greer just shakes his head and laughs at me. Then he goes outside for a smoke.

O

I've been at this temp job for a few months. I'm at home working on another painting, and it's almost time to leave for work. In my hurry to clean up, I dip the tips of my long blond hair into white paint. That's easy to squeeze out under the kitchen faucet. Drops of cerulean blue are on my black shirt, so I wet a scrubber sponge and work it off. Black is a very forgiving color when it comes to painting accidents, and that's another reason why I wear it. After cleaning my brushes, I study the painting for a few minutes before pulling myself away. I have spring fever and feel like playing hooky, but I'm heading to work.

How Do I Know?

Since there's no dress code, I'm wearing the black jeans, shirt, belt, shoes, and silver jewelry I had on when visiting my sister Helen in Southern California. Seeing all the black, she'd said, "Who the hell do you think you are—Madonna?" *No, I also wear black because I'm pale and need some contrast.* It wasn't like Helen. I'd made light of it, teasing her. "Do you mean the Virgin Mary or the Black Madonna?" She never answered.

What's going on with her? Maybe Helen was having trouble deciding whether to have children. One of my best friends let me know she was driving herself nuts trying to make this decision in her own life. *If the clock is ticking, nothing is sending signals for me.*

I snap out of this recollection. It's Friday—the high-energy day of the week—and there's a true spring bounty and a clear blue sky. Mother Nature's green plants and blooms cover the full color spectrum. Sparklers of light on indigo water outdo any mortal's creations. I don't take this beauty for granted because my view will be a nothing but a boring work screen soon.

I'm here on time, clocking in, saying hi to my boss and coworkers before sliding into my chair and turning on my computer. That's when I notice more spots of paint on my wrist and scratch them off with a fingernail.

Today is like any other Friday except a half hour into the shift, I start getting sleepy. It's not normal because it's only three thirty in the afternoon.

While doing a mental-physical health check, I find no logical reason for my sleepiness. I slept for eight hours last night. I haven't needed any allergy medication, which puts me on the ceiling or on the floor, and I haven't accepted anything from a stranger. There's a three-gallon jug of bottled water by the doorway, but I haven't helped myself to it.

Giving up on the battle to stay awake, I decide to tell my boss about my strange condition. I don't bother my coworkers, who are quietly staring at computer screens. I walk to Greer's cubicle, located near the entrance of the large room.

"What's up?" Greer knows it must be something.

I shrug and shake my head, saying, "Nothing's wrong with me, but I just can't stay awake. I'm sitting at my desk doing forward head flops."

Greer starts teasing me. "Are you serious? You've always been such a model employee."

He's the one who'd realized I'd never make it on the early-morning shift and convinced his managers to keep me on the later schedule. We have a chuckle about it.

"I *am* serious. My eyes feel so heavy and there's no reason for it. I'm fighting to stay awake. No, I'm not pregnant. Rule that out."

Greer smiles and points to the long fake wood table all the way at the other end of the room. "See those stacks of papers? How about creating some packages while standing up?"

Lucky me. "I'll give it a try," I say without any enthusiasm. *Ugh.* No one, including Greer, likes assembling packages. It's even more monotonous than the computer screen back at my desk.

The tedious repetition of this task is boring. Soon, I find myself unable to keep alert and my head starts flopping to my chest again. I can't believe it. I'm dozing even while standing. I want to curl up in a ball on the floor and just go to sleep.

This has never happened before. I try not to bother Greer again, but the urge to sleep is getting worse. I shake my head to snap out of it and make my way back to my boss's cubicle.

He's alone at his desk. My coworkers are still at theirs. Greer looks at me and says, "What's up, Wolfe? Have a seat."

"I'm here to report that nothing is helping me to stay alert—not even standing. Maybe it's narcolepsy? I'm not drugged with allergy medication that'll knock me out. I don't feel sick, but I just don't feel normal."

I sit facing him eye to eye. Before I get a chance to tell Greer that I can't perform the task, he starts talking to me, but his mouth isn't moving.

My eyes widen. This is really freaky. I stare hard at his lips to be sure. Yes, his mouth is shut and no, I'm not hallucinating.

Greer's not a ventriloquist, yet I've heard him phrase this question in a tone of disappointment tinged with slight irritation. "You mean we have to wait another week for this?"

I can't figure out how he's said this without a single movement of his lips. Plus, I have no idea what he's talking about.

Now I'm definitely awake. My gaze hasn't wavered from his face, and I swear upon everything that his lips haven't moved. I know I've heard Greer's thoughts. In the same moment, I'm alert to the fact that my boss wants me to do something.

Wait another week for this—what? My mind races to a scene from an old movie in which a teenage boy is sitting in the library listening to the thoughts of his schoolmates. Some of their mental chatter is about him. I'd found the movie odd but amusing, so the memory of it makes me smile slightly.

The sound of Greer's voice brings me back into the moment, and this time his lips *are* moving. He asks, "Walk a mile for a Camel?" His question causes me to remember telling him about the Camel cigarette case I'd found as a young girl.

Walk a mile for a Camel? Really?

What a strange thing for him to ask out of the blue.

What I don't know at this time is that Greer is using various trance techniques on me and has asked this question to interrupt my thinking.

This first interrupt technique causes my mind to immediately go into a trance state as I return to the memory of finding that Camel cigarette case.

Then Greer uses a second interrupt technique to take me out of the first trance state. He does it by jolting me into the deeper trance state that he wants me to be in. I don't know at this time that he is using mind control techniques.

How Do I Know?

I don't respond until he says, "Oman."

Oman. As soon as I hear this word, I shudder in horror, and Greer leads me out of his cubicle. I turn west to face the tall windows that run the full length of the room, and I immediately go into a trance.

My eyes roll like blinds going up. The whites show themselves to the outside world as my irises turn up into the heavens and disappear. They are fluttering rapidly, and I see nothing.

I must look like a Greek or Roman marble statue standing there with eyes revealing just a blank white area. I used to think that maybe the Greeks and Romans didn't know how to sculpt realistic eyes, but now I know it represents being in the realm of the gods.

For the first few seconds, I don't see anything. My eyes and fingers move rapidly—but not like I'm having an epileptic seizure. As my eyes flash, still revealing only the white conjunctiva, I raise my arms to feel some kind of energy that seems to be in front of me.

I stand there right in front of the window with my hands open and fingers moving as though I'm playing a complex melody on a piano. My arms move closer to my body or away from my body depending upon the intensity of whatever is coming toward me.

With eyes still fluttering, I see red, blue, and green colors flashing like lightning. Next, I sense a wind powerful enough to blow the whole world away. It feels like I'm standing in the calm area of a tornado as the scenery twists and tears everything to pieces anywhere and everywhere outside of my center's haven.

While the whites of my eyes view nothing outward, the parts of the eye turned inward continue to see the same three colors of lights flashing brilliantly. I wonder why no one in the room is responding to this violent wind.

Curiously, no one in the room is saying anything. Even my boss is silent.

My mind is in a receptive state. My upper body is still twitching when I hear an unknown male voice with some authority say, "And God made the world in seven days." It's an outer voice.

Bullshit. I say this curse word to myself in response. It's incorrect. *What are they trying to do here? Shove Christianity down my throat?*

I'm immediately annoyed since we don't actually know how we or the universe were created. After what this man said, I feel this is an attempt at brainwashing.

Seconds later, I hear another male voice, but the way it comes in is different. The tone is strange and unearthly. It speaks to my core, and its sound vibrates from inside the very center of my mind. It's an inner voice.

"Verify, verify," he says. Although it's not the voice of a human being, I'm not afraid. Once I hear him speak these two words, which sound like a special request, I respond telepathically.

Read me. As I think these words, I expand, opening up at once to allow this entity to read my soul. I feel my energy field generating a powerful charge that quickly radiates out from me like a body-encircling halo. It extends, rolling for miles, feeling like it envelops the entire planet—staying attached to me like an umbilical cord connecting me to the whole world.

Still at the window in this trance state, I feel someone approach me. I'm filled with joy because it's someone I know and love more than anyone else on earth.

My palms are touching the window now. Logically, there isn't enough space for anyone to be inside the glass, but I know this for certain—he's here because I feel this deep love like I've never experienced in this lifetime, and it's so wonderful that I just have to kiss this person. I feel my lips—and my nose too—smash up against the glass.

A few more seconds pass, and the loving feeling is replaced by feelings of horror, so I plead, silently mouthing, "Help us." I direct this back to the alien entity who asked me to "verify."

A single tear rolls from my right eye down my cheek. I beg for outside help because there is no hope for humanity to save itself from the horror coming to meet us if we do not evolve.

Moments later, I slide down the glass from the weight of the world until I'm on the floor, palms and face down. "Oh no. Oh no. No. No. No," I whisper as I rock my head from side to side on the carpeted floor.

I'm startled by the smell of my cat's urine on the carpet, knowing he would never use it as a toilet. In fact, he's at home waiting for me. The scent brings me right out of my trance like the smell of ammonia.

"Come with me, Wolfe," Greer says as he gently helps me to my feet. I want to know how long I've been at the window. "Forty-five minutes," he says.

I can't believe it because my eyes feel as though I've only blinked for a minute or so. Wouldn't they be extremely sore if they'd been fluttering wildly for that amount of time? Try it to see if I'm right.

As we walk through the hallway, I recognize the janitor who passes us. It's odd for him to be in the vicinity at this time of day. He's the same man who caught all of us dancing in the aisles one evening. When we noticed him standing in the window watching, he and everyone else laughed hysterically.

This same janitor has watched me go into and come out of a trance today. *Maybe he's here to make sure I won't run to my car and drive home.* I don't know why I have this thought.

When my boss leads me to the parking lot, no one else is here. I feel very calm and awake.

In the parking lot are two unmarked rectangular cardboard boxes about six feet high with the width and depth of a full-size refrigerator. Oddly, these have been placed side by side and are just there. I don't see a moving van or any action related to them.

My boss says nothing. Ever curious, I take a closer look and walk around to face the front of these boxes. I notice one of the boxes has a keyhole cut into it. Ignoring it, I open the box on my right, turn around to step backward into it, and then I shut its door, feeling like an ancient Egyptian entering my tomb.

How Do I Know?

No surprise—it's dark in here. I stay put, thinking, *So?*

"Wrong box," Greer says from his seated position on the curb. It's obvious—*he* knows what's going on.

Feeling foolish, I exit the first box, close its door, and move to the front of the box to my left with the keyhole. I try to open this box, but the door doesn't budge—for a reason.

Wondering what's inside, I bend down on one knee to investigate the keyhole. Looking through it, what had been flashing red, green, and blue lights flash back as technically perfect black-and-white photographs. The images present themselves one flash at a time like a slideshow. They reveal many dead men related to revolutions both political and religious.

I see Marx, Lenin, Stalin, and other Russians that I do not know by name. Then comes an image of Hitler. There are other men that I don't recognize—maybe Americans?

When I see the next two photos, I squeeze the side of the box tightly. I can't imagine why I'm seeing Jesus and John Lennon, of all people.

I see whales and sharks. A white U-shaped building appears. It has a central dome and long, narrow rectangular slits for windows. It's a view from above, and I don't get a good feeling about this image at all. The U shape means destruction in some cultures.

When there are no more images, I silently follow my boss back into the building. As we enter, I steal a glance at the glass where I'd kissed the window and notice my lip prints.

"You can go home now," says Greer, even though my shift has four hours to go. I gather my things and leave without saying anything to anyone, including my boss. I decide to never go back to that job.

Calmly, I get into my Celica GTS, buckle my seat belt, and lock the doors as always. For once I don't listen to anything and use the silence to try and comprehend what just happened to me. I also drive the actual speed limit instead of flying down the road on a highway in hell.

Once I'm home, I walk directly to the bedroom and stare at the sky from the window. I sit on the edge of the bed thinking about my new awareness and what the mind can do.

When Jared comes home, I try to explain the situation exactly as it happened—I was experimented on without my knowledge or my permission. He doesn't understand at all. Who would? It's not his fault. I don't have the vocabulary to explain it, which causes me a great deal of frustration.

Jared puts it correctly in his direct way. "I woke up at home with you and I came back home to someone else."

He's exactly right. As it happens, our relationship will never be the same again.

O

Who will understand or believe me? I wager that few people undergo such a surprising and enlightening experience while at work on a legitimate job with a detailed description of duties requiring an earthlier set of skills. *Why was I scheduled to awaken without any prior knowledge during my regular shift?*

How Do I Know?

I get fired for not returning to work, but I go back to get my final paycheck. It's fun seeing my coworkers who know nothing about my "enlightenment" incident. Nothing has changed. My lip prints are still visible on the glass. My boss jokes with me, and I act as though the previous Friday never happened. That's how I leave, and I never go back.

After being manipulated on the job by Greer, I am treated like a specimen. Every morning, my telephone rings at ten o'clock. When I answer it, there is only silence at the other end. This is different from my night visitation experience, where many callers with sweet voices left messages saying, "I love you." Even my old roommate Leila could hear it, and we'd both thought it was funny.

A friend—someone in the know—advises, "Just be careful whom you tell." Some secrets can never be told.

I didn't think there could be any verification of Judy's astonishing reading, but some of her words about energy and learning to work with it have come true.

12

THE HUSH-HUSH JOB & OTHER ADVENTURES

It's been two days since Greer's mind control techniques on April 24 at work uncorked me like a champagne bottle. It's now Opening Day on the Bay in Tiburon, California—the start of boating season, when boats of all kinds go out on the San Francisco Bay. This event has a big floating parade of decorated boats and yacht club races later in the day.

"You can get on any boat honey—they'll take you," says an exuberant woman who pokes her head in my car window.

Barbara and I look at each other and laugh. "That sounds like fun. I love the water!" Barbara exclaims.

"It's good you're early because you can park right over there." The woman points to a lot up ahead.

We have two choices: this event or an art and music fair. The feeling of being exploded out of my own bottle like an enormous genie who'll never fit back in makes me want to get as close as I can to a big body of water like the bay or an ocean. "Let's head for the water," I say to Barbara, who has asked me to choose.

My sunroof is open, and it's another beautiful day until we drive into the Tiburon public parking lot. We see six men wearing police uniforms surrounding a midnight-blue Celica in an almost empty area of the lot. It looks exactly like mine.

Although I park my car away from the other Celica, something awful hits and a shock of horror travels through me. An agonizing splitting pain goes into my head and neck at the same time. I duck to protect myself from the horrible sensation of bullets entering my brain.

It's unbelievable how Barbara doesn't even notice my head and upper body crammed down next to the steering wheel. She's still cheerfully chatting away and oblivious to what I'm feeling.

My heart pounds and my whole body is shaking. I fight the fear to stay in control of my senses and attempt to stifle my gasps. Finally, the pain leaves. I'm still alive, and even that's puzzling. Once I'm able to breathe, I want to get out.

It's the unusual growl in my voice that catches Barbara by surprise—plus I've cut her off midsentence, so she gives me a startled look followed by a worried frown because she's never heard me bark before.

"Wait here, and don't move until I come back. I'll explain," I tell her. There is dead silence.

I'm full of adrenaline, and my senses are heightened. I force myself to get out of the car slowly because I have to know what just happened and why. I don't want to move too fast when heading over to the rear of that Celica where the police are gathered around. I'm apprehensive because I think maybe I shouldn't approach them right in the middle of—I don't know what.

I don't get too close. I don't want to get in the way or cause any alarm. I choose the friendliest-looking officer. "What's going on?" I ask in a gentle tone. His eyes shift away from the Toyota to me. He looks at me like he's sizing me up first before answering. *Maybe he heard my car door shut and knows that I've just gotten out of an identical Toyota.*

"You don't want to know. It would ruin your day." He sounds protective and doesn't divulge anything.

I stand firm, tilt my head, and look quizzically at this officer. He reads a question in my body language: *Why?*

The other policemen look at me but don't add anything. They let the first officer have his say. "There's a dead body in the trunk with bullets to the head and neck. This individual has been murdered," he informs me.

"Oh," I reply. I just nod matter-of-factly. He must have sensed I could handle this kind of information. *Well, I'm wearing black jeans and a motorcycle jacket—not a dress.*

Although I want to see the body, I don't ask if I can. *Ugh, the body was stuffed in the trunk first and then murdered.* I feel like vomiting when I realize that I have a newly acquired ability to feel exactly how the victim feels and dies. This policeman doesn't know he's just verified the

peculiar way I've already gotten the same information. "Thank you."
Thank you more than you'll ever know. I get it now.

As I think on this, I tremble with gratitude and feel lucky I
arrived after the first Celica. Maybe I could have been mistaken for the
person who was murdered since we have twin cars. The negative feelings
this experience causes are hard to shake off. *As if being mind-tested at
my job on Friday wasn't bad enough—now this too? Happy Sunday. I
just want to get out of here.*

Another shiver goes through me as I get back in the car. "I didn't
mean to be rude and cut you off earlier. It's because, well, you aren't
going to believe what just happened," I say to Barbara. I tell her what I
learned and hope she's not too shocked.

"I can't imagine how you must feel. It's creepy. The victim's car
looks like yours too. Whoa. What a coincidence," says Barbara.

It's a relief that she's open to what I've said. So, I also tell her, "I
felt the violence as soon as we drove into the parking lot and I saw the
car. It's like being slimed with the murder because this horrible feeling is
still on me. Can we get out of here and go to the beach?"

"I'm fine with that. I know a beautiful beach—Limantour. I'll
show you how to get there."

We're silent for a bit as we head out of Tiburon, and I hope
Barbara's not disappointed by the way this day is turning out. She's my
first new age—really old age—acquaintance. Somehow, she understands
what I don't have the language for, and she's very supportive, like an old
friend. With Jared, I might as well be speaking in a foreign tongue.

Although I'm trying to comprehend what happened at work, something else is new too—I'm now one angry gal.

Limantour Beach is beautiful—nice and flat. But it's foggy. That's probably why we're the only ones here. Barbara and I take off our shoes and walk along the shore just where the end of a wave barely slides over the sand. We look for shells and other gifts from the ocean.

"It's still a gorgeous day here even with a little fog. The atmosphere feels magical," Barbara says. "I see a family with a dog— way down there to the right."

"Yes, I can barely see them. They look like painterly phantoms." My gaze returns to the water. "This is more like an East Coast beach than any of the other California beaches I've seen, the way the waves come in."

Barbara puts a hand to her forehead to hold back her pale strawberry-blond hair as she looks out toward the ocean. The breeze is whipping her long tresses, and she turns to keep them from blowing across her mouth when she speaks. "I love swimming here. It's one of the safest and prettiest beaches around."

"So, no riptides? I feel like jumping in the ocean. I've had this big urge ever since Friday and especially after feeling a murder today." I look over at Barbara in her jean jacket, T-shirt, and shorts. "Are you cold?" I ask.

"No, I'm fine. It feels kind of balmy to me. I'm used to the Northern California weather because I was born here. This is where I like to go kayaking because there's no undertow."

"Are you a surfer dudette too?" I ask. Barbara has a laid-back nature-girl quality—maybe it's just being a Californian.

"No." Barbara giggles. "But I'm a swimmer. Lakes, pools, rivers, waterslides—wherever there's water, I'm in."

"How about right now?" Although I'm serious, I laugh. "I have to jump in. I don't care if I don't have a swimsuit."

"Well, the nude beach is at the other end." Now Barbara laughs.

"Oh, I'm thinking of jumping in right here with all my clothes on—motorcycle jacket and all," I say. "I'll leave my shoes on the beach, though. I do want to go home with them."

"You're serious," Barbara says. She raises one sandy-colored eyebrow more than the other, and her forehead wrinkles a little.

"I am," I say, tossing my studded pointy-toe shoes and sunglasses onto the sand well above the waterline. "I have to—right now." I zip the breast pocket of my leather jacket closed so I don't lose my car keys, and then I prove my words by heading for the water.

"Okay. Wait—I am too." Barbara chuckles as she throws her shoes near mine and buttons up her blue jean jacket. I can't believe Barbara is going to jump in to give me moral support, but she's running for the water and catches up.

"It's cold, but I don't care!" I shriek into the breeze as I hop through the little waves and into the surf.

"You're not kidding." Barbara shivers as we slosh through knee-deep waves. She clutches her jean jacket and turns as the water crashes at our waists.

"I have to get all the way in," I yell to Barbara just before the next wave crests. I dive headfirst beneath the water and into powerful Mami Wata (Mother Water) territory. What a rush and a remedy. It only takes an instant to feel washed with relief.

When I pop back up, I look around for Barbara. She comes up out of the water and whips her head back to keep her hair out of the way. When she sees me, we laugh hysterically because we're just a couple of bobbing heads.

The water temperature is unbelievable. It feels like swimming in snow, and it's hard to talk when we start to shiver. "We did it!" I exclaim. "It's cold as hell—did—you know—hell's not hot? Are my lips blue yet?"

Barbara laughs at this and crosses her arms in front of her. "God, it's freezing," she cries.

"I'll race you out of here." I shiver. "It's hard work dragging these wet clothes through the waves."

Barbara and I stagger out of the surf. "Trying to run on sand in wet clothes feels terrible," she yells.

We grab our shoes, still laughing like fools. The air doesn't feel much warmer than the water as we run for the car.

"No plan, no towels, no dry clothes—but there's heat," I say as we both get in.

"I can't believe we just did that. And you jumped in wearing that leather jacket." She laughs.

"Makeshift wetsuit—spur of the moment. Pretty good, huh?" We keep giggling at the ridiculousness of it all. "Thanks for coming with me. I just had to head for water, and I don't know why exactly. I'm glad it was the ocean—what a relief."

"That was some cra-a-zy fun," says Barbara, still shivering. She adjusts the vent. "Is this Easter Sunday?"

"Ha ha. You're a good Catholic. I think it was last week. You might feel warmer without your jean jacket. Aim all those vents right toward you. This leather is protecting me from the cold air, so go for it."

"Here comes the heat. Can you believe it—nobody's on the road," says Barbara. "Whoops. Wrong."

A single car is heading toward us on the two-lane back road. The light's just right. Without the blaring sun, I can see clearly. "Look, look. Is that—it can't be. It looks like Greer's vintage car."

"Huh? It does. He's singing. No, he's not. It looks like he's yelling. What a twisted, angry face. Wow, that guy's upset," notes Barbara, turning as he passes by.

We've both observed him. I try, but I can't read the license plate in the rearview mirror to be sure. "If it's Greer, he *should* be upset," I say.

"I think Greer liked you."

A. Wolfe

There's no point in talking about him, I think. *He really screwed up by playing with me like that. I don't care to hear anything about him or that job.*

When I'm quiet, Barbara asks, "How do you feel?"

How I feel is a loaded question. "You mean after today or Friday?" I sigh.

"Both. Don't worry. I'm not saying anything to anyone at work. As a matter of fact, I'm thinking of quitting myself."

"I'm okay," I tell her, keeping what happened mostly to myself. "Some good advice was given to me by a psychic. She said, 'You have to learn how to keep the negative away.'" Feeling grateful, I add, "Well, I can't thank you enough for helping me by leaving Tiburon. Right now, I feel tons lighter. Thanks for being here."

Barbara places a supportive hand on my arm, squeezing it lightly. "You're welcome," she says, and her face lights up. "Oh, by the way, since you're not working right now, there's a great bookstore in Sausalito you might want to visit. It's the only one on the main street and it has a lot of psychic info."

"That's good to know."

O

It doesn't take long to get to Sausalito when tailing the end of the Monday rush hour traffic heading to San Francisco.

Exploring the beautiful downtown, I notice two men standing

226

inside a small shop with their backs to the storefront. With their profiles visible, this makes me just outside their peripheral vision. As I pass by the glass window, a sign over the doorway—Visions Bookstore—catches my attention, and that's why I decide to go in. There they are, leaning against the front counter, hovering over a large book.

Both of them are so engrossed in what they're doing that when I open the front door, neither one hears me come in. Their heads are almost touching. The older man adjusts his gold round-rimmed glasses with a thumb and forefinger before pointing and tapping various places on the page. It looks like the younger man is performing a blessing when he lowers and raises his hand over the same page as if he's following the older man's pattern.

"Do you feel that?" says the solidly built younger man. He cocks his head toward the older man as though he wants to get some kind of verification about their tapping and waving—like they've just worked some ritual magic right there in the bookstore.

The older man adjusts the cuffs of his pale patterned white shirt and shrugs. When he shakes his head to indicate that he's felt nothing, the young man spins around on one heel to locate the source himself. I notice his almost imperceptible nod when our eyes meet, and then he turns back around without a word.

I know it's me he feels. I'm aware of it too. It's not easy to explain how I extend out further now—ever since being the subject experimented on few days ago. Let's just say a new addition is part of me and now I'm doing my own testing instead of being tested.

The feeling is like having a long train of awareness attached that doesn't just trail behind me as I walk. It's also moving from some future train. In the beginning, it's probably best to stand in the stationary position of now until I get my bearings. This would be the area of X marks the spot on a sideways eight—the infinity symbol.

A manual on how to use these new abilities could be around here somewhere. I haven't taken a forward step since I entered the store because I don't know where to start looking. *Religion, goddess, psychic, occult, metaphysical, ESP, parapsychology—so many subjects—putting all of this together might take forever.*

The older man with his trimmed beard and matching gray hair notices me. "I'm the owner of this bookstore. Let me know if you're looking for anything in particular," he says with a friendly, welcoming voice.

I end up nodding to both of them because the young man has turned around again. They get back to their conversation and I begin my search on the left side of the store. *I'm after books on how occult energy works.*

The two men don't stop their conversation, and I listen while looking at book titles. They start talking about what I'm looking for, and that lures me away from the bookshelves. I pause my search and head to the counter to join them.

We're still the only ones in the store, and now all three of us are having a conversation. I observe that the owner has a lot of occult information, while the younger man has something else. This is what attracted me to their conversation, and they don't mind at all that I've sort of butted my way into it.

How Do I Know?

Is this the man I'm supposed to meet? He's bright, strong, and self-assured with something familiar I can't place.

"I know I've been a monk before," he suddenly says, as though he's at odds with his own information.

"Don't feel bad—I've been a guy before." I laugh. I'm impressed because I've never met someone who has seen the people he's been. "This could be too weird . . ." I trail off. *Maybe I shouldn't . . .*

"Keep talking," says the young man. He's resting against the counter with an arm dangling over it and his legs crossed at the ankles. He means it because his gaze doesn't shift away.

Encouraged but still hesitant, I begin. "It's scary. I had an unexpected shift in my vision, where suddenly people looked like there was no life behind their eyes. I mean they looked unaware, like they were dead. It was so creepy that I had to leave and go back home. I call it my vampire experience."

"I've had that," he replies, not even hesitating, so I believe him.

"It's not something to bring up first because there's no way to say it without sounding nuts," I say, giving him my jokey look. "I'm just telling you since you've been a monk."

When he smiles, his cheeks dimple and his eyes express that he already knows. "I understand. I believe you because I've had this experience too."

Our conversation stops when a customer comes in with a list of books for the owner. "Go ahead," says the young man to the woman. He nods to the owner and then he looks at me. "Care to walk with me? It's bold of me to ask, but I want to talk to you some more. I need to feed the meter—it's not far."

"Sure," I say. "I'm enjoying our conversation." He opens the door for me, and we head out along the main street of this scenic waterfront city.

"I'm Jamie by the way. I'm visiting from the East Coast and leaving today. Is there some way we can keep talking?" His voice has a tone of regret.

"I'm from the East Coast too, but now I live here with my boyfriend. He's not the jealous type—he knows I love him. We'll keep in touch. Yes, I'd like that. There'll be more time for me to tell you about my reading. A psychic told me that I'd been a man before, and I knew she could see because I saw that when I was in elementary school."

"A psychic? We don't have anyone like that where I live," he says enthusiastically. "If you ever see her again, could you ask her something for me? I know I've been a monk."

"I will. I won't forget either," I say, wishing he didn't have to leave today.

"I've never talked to anyone like you. I really would like to keep in touch."

"I thought I was the only one in the world." I sighed, feeling my burden of responsibility shift.

I'm not the only one feeling emotional about it. "What did I do to you last lifetime so that we're so far apart in age?" Jamie exclaims as though he carries some secret guilt.

"You didn't do anything wrong," I assure him.

Jamie and I exchange our info. Before he gets in the car to leave, we hug like we never want to let go of each other. It's a hug of realizing that we are alike and the only ones of our kind that we've met here on earth.

O

Jamie calls and calls for about two weeks until finally, I answer. I don't regret picking up the phone.

He writes to me, and I like that about a man—ever since David, my first love, who wrote love letters with poems, jokes, cartoons, and original art. "Hello, Kiddo" is how Jamie's letters often begin.

One day Jamie calls and his first words are a question. "Why do I see a picture of a scared cat?"

"I can't get anything by you. I just mailed a letter with a photo of my cat. He's afraid of cameras and it really shows. You'll see when you get it."

Just over a month later, I call Jamie with some news. "Do you have a minute? Get ready for this—you might want to sit down."

"You saw her?" he asks.

Is that a good guess or does Jamie know? I bet he knows.

"Wow. You're more than good. You are correct and you were right about . . ." I let my words hang unfinished.

"Go ahead. Tell me. I won't interrupt." Jamie's voice has that same excitement and strength, just like the time he asked the bookstore owner, "Do you feel that?"

"Well, I asked the psychic if she could give me some information about you, and all she needed was your age, hair color, and location. I told her nineteen, dark brown, and exactly where you live on the East Coast. Within seconds, Judy said, 'He's been a monk before. He's taken vows of silence.'"

"I knew it," Jamie whispers under his breath. When I chuckle, he says, "I guess you heard that."

"I know how that feels. We received our own previous life information first. Then, the same psychic tells us what we already know, and none of this can be confirmed scientifically yet," I say.

"Ha ha. We're ahead of science. Even though I saw myself as a monk, it's a relief to have it verified. I didn't have to ask or even be there. She's good."

"There's more," I say. "You and I were paired as temple brother and sister in Egypt when the temple was equal. We went into other cultures to do our work, almost like missionaries. And we even got married—only because it was part of the culture we entered. Judy also said that few people on this planet can beat your psychic abilities. She didn't say how children were chosen or paired, and I didn't think to ask her."

"What did I do to you last lifetime so that we're not together this lifetime?" Jamie asks again.

"Judy never mentioned anything negative about our past. If you did something terrible, I would probably feel it," I reassure him. I wonder where this guilt is coming from.

"I hope not," he says sincerely. "It means a lot to finally have someone to talk to . . ."

"It's a relief for me. We must still feel the influence of Egypt's ancient temple training. Their priests and priestesses were known far and wide for their abilities," I tell him.

"That's how I'm able to interfere with the TV. My brother doesn't know it's me. He fixes it and I create the interference again."

"Oh, poor brother. That's funny. It's not the big whales you have to worry about—it's the little whales."

"What do you mean?" Jamie asks, sounding concerned.

"Oh, I'm just teasing you. I know you don't only have a destructive hand," I say, feeling certain about it.

"You're right. I helped a woman get out of coma once. I checked her colors first and did healing work on her. She was mad at me when she came back, though. I think it's because she wanted to pass on." He sounds disappointed.

"I think I understand what you mean. Once, I was visiting a hospital and walked by the room of a woman who was just sitting there.

She looked out of touch, and I'd never seen anyone so dazed. There was a framed photograph on the bedside table, and I assumed it was someone she loved. For some reason, I picked it up and rushed it toward her face. After shoving it right in front of her, the woman's entire focus changed. She was back to normal, aware of her surroundings, and speaking. It was amazing. I was so young that I can't tell you what was wrong with her or what I did exactly."

"You pushed her back home." Jamie chuckles. "Back in her body."

"You must be right because that's how it looked. Okay, time to get back to it. When I finish this painting, I'll send you a photo."

"You're leaving me in suspense. Well, Kiddo, I'll call you next week."

"Okay, and no peeking. I want to surprise you. To be continued," I joke.

"B-b-b-bye." I hear Jamie's chuckle before hanging up.

O

I've been lucky to meet Barbara, and now Jamie. I'm not a freak or a specimen to them. There are some peculiar insights I can never say anything about—nothing new. That part is just as it's always been. *Well, this irregular gal will be seeing a regular girlfriend shortly—no problem.*

Lauren and I are out on one of our escapades the day the agency phones me with another assignment. She's homesick for some English food, so we're having a lunch for the cure—eating bangers and drinking John Courage beer—a first for me.

Due to the unaccountable work incident, I'm not in any hurry to get a new job. But it has the same afternoon hours as my old job, which gives me more daytime to do what I want before heading to work, so I accept the offer.

Lauren's musician husband is a longtime friend of my boyfriend, Jared. It was after visiting them a few times that he and I decided to move from Silicon Valley. These newlyweds know the area, and Lauren's been showing me around. She and I hit it off like our male counterparts, and we pal around since we both have time earlier in the day.

We plan to head to the beach after lunch even though my new assignment starts this very day. Lauren and I have our swimsuits on under our pretty cover-up dresses.

"My gram was showing off her legs at our wedding while telling everyone a joke about how these are the last parts to go downhill. Our guests were in hysterics watching her dance because to look at her— she's a proper lady. I'm calling her early tomorrow. I miss her humor." Lauren smiles wistfully for a moment, still rubbing her wedding ring.

Lauren's wedding story reminds me of my own grandmother. "I would love it if Mama did something like that, but I can't even imagine it. My uncles took me aside and showed me a framed photograph of Mama in her long wedding gown with petals like a lily for the hem. Word traveled that she was a smart beauty, and men came from all over the state just to woo her. She was stunning." I glance down at the aquamarine and diamond ring that Jared gave me. *Wedding?* A nervous shudder zooms through my body. *I'd have to be carried down the aisle on a stretcher.*

After taking the last sip of John Courage, I compliment my new friend to uplift her. "Well, a good sense of humor must run in your family. It looks like beauty and great legs do too."

Lauren flips her long blond hair and says, "Thank you for that and for indulging my wish for some pub food."

"I get to say I've eaten a good banger, and it's far larger than a hotdog. Now, I dare you to dance like your gram on the way out. I'll do it if you do." I encourage Lauren by bouncing up and down.

"Agreed," she says. "Let's shake it on out of here." We hear applause, laughs, and whistles from the easygoing pub staff behind us.

The Pacific Ocean is too cold for a swim, but we California transplants still have fun walking along the beach. It must be a real culture shock for Lauren to come to America. Just moving across country took some adjusting for me.

Despite today's adventure, something's bugging me. "Do you mind if we drive by the building where my new job is located on the way back?" I ask.

"Of course not." Lauren adjusts the passenger seat so she can stretch out her long legs.

"I won't work just anywhere," I banter, not revealing that this is a reconnaissance run—just in case.

How Do I Know?

Lauren is different from my close girlfriends—not eccentric or creative. She's more down to earth. If I mention psychics or the paranormal, Lauren's mind closes. For instance, yesterday I was driving on a curvy back road for the second time—it was a shortcut Lauren showed me. I noticed an intersection street sign with two different street names on it, and the one with Lauren's last name seemed to jump right at me. I couldn't ignore the odd way it popped out to grab my attention. It sprang slightly forward and then rippled like water was washing over it. It seemed impossible, but it happened for a reason. I made sure to note the time. It happened at twelve o'clock straight up.

When I got home, I called Lauren before checking my messages. "By the way, did you call me at noon?" I asked.

"That's exactly when I called you!" she exclaimed.

Too bad Lauren wouldn't understand how she helped me solve the mystery of what waved and winked at me on Wolfe Grade Road. Yes, it is weird, but it's physics—even if its time-space action did appear like a distorted cartoon. I hid my amusement.

The turn is coming. "Our destination is the driveway on the right," I announce, heading for the entrance.

"I'm impressed. This is quite the welcome," quips Lauren as the building's alarm system sounds and the sprinklers turn on.

Immediately, a nicely dressed blond man comes out through the front door and stands in the manner of a sentry. He's clean cut and looks about thirty-five.

"Who is this guy wearing a suit?" I ask. "He's obviously not the maintenance man."

"Very posh. Valet service too?" Lauren is in rare form. She straightens up to get a better look.

There is something odd about the way this man has hurried out of the building to stand there like a watcher. Don't rush to conclusions. He's probably a smoker.

I expect him to light a cigarette any second. When he doesn't, I'm suspicious—thanks to my last job.

Did he trip the alarm to warn the others in case I come in now instead of at three o'clock?

"We're closer to the building, so I'll slow way down. Let's get a better look at him." Behind my gray alien-eye-shaped sunglasses, I can pretend that I'm looking left and not at him. "I really don't know what to make of this guy," I say to Lauren, hoping to get her read. "He looks out of place. What do you think he's doing?"

"He's not having a fa—I mean a smoke. He appears too well dressed to take care of the sprinkler system that's gone off, and he's just ignoring the alarm. Very unfriendly-looking face, as though he's blaming us for the malfunctioning equipment." Lauren confirms just what I've been thinking.

"He seems very nosy, and I don't like that expression of his either," I add.

"Sod off," Lauren says when we pass him on the way out of the parking lot.

"Have a wet sod." I'm not sure what I'm saying. *I hope he's not here when I come back.*

This whole incident is amusing on the outside, but it's not funny inside to me. We shake our heads and giggle as we leave the parking lot and head to Lauren's house. "Let me know how it goes," she says.

"Maybe I should go to work wearing my swimsuit and cover-up in case the sprinklers go off again." I laugh.

"That's completely bonkers—I love it," says Lauren. "We'll talk."

After dropping her off, I head home to change into jeans and a T-shirt. *No one said anything about a dress code.*

A little later, I'm driving into the same parking lot—no fanfare, no alarm, no sprinkler system. I wonder if it was an early warning about the job.

There's no sign of sour guy as I walk into the featureless grid building. *Hmm.* There are no plants, photos, posters, or paintings inside, but there are no unpacked boxes either. Something about it seems fake. There's dead air in here. I feel it as soon as I walk into this sterile place, which makes me want to turn around and leave.

"You're the new hire?" A cold, uninterested expression crosses the woman's face, and her monotone voice is dull like her dark blue suit, which looks almost like a uniform. She wears no jewelry or anything to suggest a personal style. Her white hands look stony, and the way she's clutching a stack of papers has drained the blood out of her fingers.

What a stiff with no personality. I don't think I've ever met such a person. She's as unfriendly as that man in the parking lot earlier.

The woman explains my responsibilities as though she's tired of repeating them. "You'll be working with these files, verifying military bills of lading." Blah, blah, and blah—she goes on about the process with an abbreviated way of speaking—no full sentences.

"Sure, I can handle it," I tell her. *Yuck.* I see she's even wearing unflattering flats when she walks away. *Stop it. Don't be the face of ugly,* I scold myself. *You have to learn to keep the negative away from you.* Judy's words echo like she's speaking to me.

My intuition is telling me this work with military bills of lading isn't exactly a real job situation. Something phony's going on here. I know the staff isn't leveling with me.

The next day, I still don't have any concrete proof anything's amiss, but something's up. *Maybe these are phony bills of lading.* The environment is terrible, and it has the feel of a hush-hush job.

My second shift isn't even over, but my intuition is almost yelling that it's time to leave. Even my headset's reception is bad. It's so full of static that I can't tune in to anything to tune out the job, which annoys me.

"Can't get your radio station?" my supervisor asks with delight. *How does she know? She can't hear it.* Her phony tone makes me want to flip her the bird.

There's something about the people here that makes me feel unsociable, which is rare for me. I try focusing on work to forget about the last job, where I was a guinea pig for someone's psychic experiment. Yes, doesn't it sound crazy?

I'm not concentrating until I read the name A. Quirk on a file. Immediately, I think of elementary quark particles and try to forget about the boring work at hand. But my intuition keeps urging me to go. *Go— something's going on here and it's not right.*

I pick up A. Quirk's unfinished file and shove it violently back into its place on the wall of folders. Then I walk out of the building and into some fresh air.

It feels good just to get away from that office building. In front of a flagpole, I let it rip. "Fuck you!" I scream at the top of my lungs, jumping and spitting like an angry llama.

This is when I notice a man with a long brown ponytail walking on the sidewalk. He's calmly heading right toward me. He doesn't look like the dull, dead bunch I've left behind. "I hope my foul language didn't offend you," I say, now feeling silly because I wasn't directing my anger at him.

"I didn't hear anything at all," says the man in a measured tone of voice. He looks pleased. This makes me angry because I know he's lying—he's not deaf.

Oh, read between the lines. Fuck anything and everything. I probably take his answer the wrong way, but I yell, "Fuck you!" again.

Well, I saw a sour blond man when I came here. He looked out of place. Now I see a ponytailed man as I'm leaving, and I'm not sure of his place either. The first man—he was definitely part of the hush-hush.

Okay. So, I just spit in front of the American flag. Would I be dissected by now if I were in some other country in this primitive world? Do not ask me to work for you. I will never work for you. This eyeball has left the building.

I don't go back.

O

My telephone still rings every day around ten o'clock and I still answer it. I know it's not the agency, and I know there will be no one on the line. I'm right. This is the way it is—I'm just a specimen.

A few minutes after ten, Barbara drops by to visit and tells me about her living situation with her roommate. When she explains what's going on, her toothy smile turns into a frown. "My roommate is acting like a jerk for no good reason." She sighs in frustration and stops. As her mouth twists into a tight grimace, her eyes fill with tears. "We've been friends for years. Everything was fine and we didn't have any issues. Now she's turned into one jealous and controlling bitch."

"You can't live around that, and you don't deserve to be treated that way. It sounds like she's going through some personal changes and she's blaming you when it's not your fault." Barbara is a gentle and considerate person. She has my support. "I'm calling Jared right now to ask if you can stay with us. Help yourself to some tea or coffee." In no time, I get his answer. "It's okay with Jared. My sweet man didn't even hesitate when I asked if you could stay with us for a while."

Barbara's tense face transforms. Her clenched jaw relaxes and her eyes crinkle with happiness as she gives me a hug. "Thanks for your help." Then she hangs her head as though embarrassed by the whole thing. "I'll just stay until I find my own place," she assures me.

"We aren't going to charge you anything, so you can save some money. Don't worry. I'll give you a key to our place so you can use the kitchen and bathroom—it'll work out just fine."

It doesn't take Barbara long to move in. She's just settling into our upstairs garage, which is like a bedroom with a closet, lots of shelves, and a rectangular window with a beautiful view of Mount Tamalpais.

Now, it's late. Jared and I have already watched some late-night comedy in our cozy bed and the TV's off. Usually, I'm the one to fall asleep within minutes, but he's asleep and I'm beside him awake and fuming.

Judy's words echo. *You could focus your mind and your will. Things appeared out of thin air. It's not something that is done today.*

"Why not? If there's no such thing as time," I hiss under my breath.

I decide to experiment, although I don't know how long to concentrate on creating a cloud. These things don't operate on clock time. As I put my thoughts into making it, I pull my cloud image along—dragging it like striking a match.

Since I haven't first cleared my mind of the anger and frustration I feel toward certain individuals on both jobs, my recipe with these emotions also moves with the cloud like an additional formula. I focus my attention and use my will on the cloud until I fall asleep.

Jared's left for work. I'm already dressed and in the kitchen when I hear a soft knock at the door.

Balancing a cup of coffee, I open it. "Good morning, roommate. How are you sleeping? I worry that the pebbled floor may not be comfortable enough."

Barbara stands there with her toiletry bag, clothes, and a towel. "I'm fine, but I might buy an air mattress. By the way, it rained last night."

"Oh? It did? There wasn't any rain in the forecast."

"That's right—I heard that. Rainfall is rare in the summer, but there was a storm last night. I saw it from the window. It was weird because it was the dirtiest, angriest, dustiest raincloud I've ever seen."

Good. It worked. "Do you want to go for a hike after you get dressed and eat some breakfast?"

"That would be great. It's a beautiful day."

We glide with the sun coming through the windshield and land a parking spot without a big hunt for one. Grabbing our packs, we head for the park.

"That was easy." Barbara twists her hair into a messy bedhead bun as we walk along.

"Thank you," I say to the inconceivable when looking up at a sky filtered by my sunglasses. I adjust the pack on my back, feeling grateful.

"Greer asked about you. I didn't give him any info," says Barbara, who still works there.

"Thanks for not saying anything." I don't say another word about it and change the subject. "A funny thing—last night the name Diana kept coming to me. I wonder if I should change my name to Diana. A name with more than one syllable is appealing, but will I answer to anything else but my birth name? What do you think?" I try it out, saying, "My name is Diana."

"I like it. Look at that blond guy straight ahead. It looks like he's waving to us."

"Do you know him?" I ask.

"Diana! Diana!" he yells, waving to get our attention.

"No, but he thinks he knows you." Barbara chuckles. "Wow, there are no accidents."

"Is this funny or what?" I oblige the stranger by waving back as though I'm the Diana he thinks he's seeing. "Ha ha, he really thinks I'm Diana."

"I see. Well, that answers that," teases Barbara.

Me, me, me. I, I, I. While I'm in all my stories, they're more about my weird experiences. This is how I got the name Diana and why I'm using it here.

What's weird is that ever since being pried open by Greer, I either dream reality or think reality ahead of time. Then the event occurs.

It's like my awareness is living in the world of the unconscious mind.

O

Months later, it's the twentieth anniversary of the Summer of Love Festival on Haight Street in San Francisco—like a shift to the past. Sandalwood and cannabis scents fill the air as they did when nearly one hundred thousand people showed up to create the original social phenomenon.

My good friend Steffie and I stroll past vendors selling unusual items along with artists, craftspeople, and jewelers. Stages have been set up in the middle of the street for the bands to play. On either side of the street are vintage clothing shops, music stores, sixties stores, restaurants, smoke shops, and nightclubs.

People dress however they want—even in costume like its Halloween—and are all accepted. The easygoing crowd is here to have fun.

I'm behind Steffie in the middle of the street when a white butterfly swoops into a circle of empty space in front of me and hovers a few yards away. *I wonder if I can pull it toward me.* Yes, what a crazy thought, but why not try and see?

The procedure? *Focus on it and drag it.* This is what I do—like reaching out with an invisible hand. It's working. The creature starts flapping toward me and lands on my nose like it's the biggest perch around.

I have to show Steffie, but how can I say her name without blowing it off? "Steffie. Steffie," I call from one side of my mouth.

How Do I Know?

She hears me and turns around. "Ha ha ha," she bellows when she sees it on my nose.

When two guys walking in front of us hear her roaring with laughter, they turn around to see what's so funny. "You're the goddess of the summer of love," they both proclaim, and they start laughing too.

I grin at their laughter with the hope of keeping the creature on my nose a little bit longer. The white butterfly slightly opens and closes its wings and then stops. This is its pattern the whole time.

I'm amazed. My secret experiment worked. Or did it? My wish could be an amusing coincidence, but it's an uncanny thing. There must be something or someone behind the scenes—a good helper in the breeze maybe.

Don't look down on any source. This is my motto. And even a butterfly can be a messenger.

13

DEAR WORSE-A-DOODLE

Dear Worse-A-Doodle,

What I'm about to tell you will sound like fiction, but this is a true tale of tracking patterns and chasing down a foretelling—better known as a prophecy. There is no fast and easy way to explain it, so please be patient. You'll begin to see its reality as you read on. Once you've finished, if you need further proof to verify what I've written, ask the wisest person you know to read you.

My story starts with a boy who came to visit me. When I became aware of him, I was just a few years into this life in my new body. He said his name was Worse-A-Doodle, and while his name is unusual, he was familiar to me.

How Do I Know?

Yes, it was Worse-A-Doodle who found me when I was a three-year-old. He was already in school, but the fact that I couldn't read yet didn't matter to either of us. He was my first friend, and he was not like any other person I knew—especially the way he showed up. We are different in the same way, and even though we may not recognize each other now, we will.

He might remember what we talked about, but I was so young I can't recall our conversations—only his name. I could go back to my thinking at the time about what was important in my life—that's probably what he and I talked about. I fed him more with friendship than with the big soupspoon I carried to the pantry where we met.

I took three secrets with me when our family moved two states away to another home that was next door to a church. Its religion didn't interest me because I was already reading another religion—Greek mythology—and it was more exciting. I only enjoyed the popular family-night buffet dinner held monthly in the church's large reception room.

One summer during family night when I was twelve, I wore the gold wedding band my first elementary school boyfriend slipped onto my finger in the church. When he and his family moved because his officer father got stationed someplace new, I missed his companionship.

As usual, the adults pushed me to the head of the buffet line just because I was skinny and they wanted to fatten me up. They didn't know I had an appetite like my uncle, who was once asked to leave an all-you-can-eat place.

My mother had relayed the nutritional information she learned in college, and it made sense, so that night I first filled up on four or five helpings of healthy foods from the many dishes and platters placed on six tables. Despite lots of refills, I didn't skip the desserts, even though sugar was banned in our house except for holidays and birthdays. I tell you this so you don't think that eating too much was the main reason for what happened to me at family night.

After our big dinner, the long brown floor-to-ceiling accordion divider was pulled closed, cutting the large reception room in half. On one side, the adults sat in rows of chairs facing a white screen. They watched slideshows in the dark as they listened to missionaries talk about their work around the world.

We children were more interested in socializing, so the lights stayed on in our half of the room with the kitchen. The way the tables and chairs were set up for us created a wide middle aisle from one end of the long room to the other.

There were plenty of art supplies—colored pencils, crayons, and paper. Our project was to design and test aircraft that had nothing to do with church unless you count the ETs in a spaceship spotted by the prophet Ezekiel.

Humans, animals, or designs were drawn on most of our planes. Some had logos, and a few were simply folded without any personal color treatment. When our planes were finished, there was a flying competition. We sat still for each maiden flight because every plane had to fly on its own without any interference or it would be disqualified.

Worse-A-Doodle, you found me there that night just like when you first visited years earlier. I don't know how you did because this time I wasn't home.

How Do I Know?

I guess you couldn't resist the perfectly designed plane my friend hurled into the air—the first one being judged by all of us. It was heading straight for me to catch, but you intercepted it, shifting its flight. That's the moment I saw what looked like you—pale and shimmering ahead to the right. Then both the plane and the room went sideways, and I veered onto the floor.

The way you plucked the craft pulled me into the same sphere as you, where light flashes just like it does inside a dream. I had a glimpse for a few seconds before everything went black and then blank.

Then there was nothing but intermittent brightness. Were you waving over me, breaking into this constant light? I felt something on my face. "Get her mother!" a girl yelled.

The room divider must have opened because all I saw next were heads—my mother, the minister, and my friend—all hovering over me with their hair, faces, and noses pointing at me. There they were, but why?

There was a sound like water dripping. It was one hand slapping me. It belonged to my friend who threw the plane. "She fainted," said the girl, even though there was nothing to confirm it. Finally, she stopped giving me pinker cheeks.

Groups of smaller heads were now stuffed into every empty space between the large adult heads. My friend's was in the center. Many curious eyes stared like they were all part of one head with a single brain trying to figure out what was going on.

I was conscious enough to know that I was flat on my back on the floor, but I didn't accept that I'd only fainted—not after seeing you reach for that plane to change its trajectory. There's no way the plane could have made such an immediate sideways movement on its own without a strong wind.

Everything would be fine, and I'd have clearer images of you if these hadn't been slapped out of me. I wonder if all that commotion caused you to leave in hurry. Or maybe it disturbed the field surrounding you? All I know is that you were there.

It's curious. When I rewind the time to review this incident, I see you in some ghostly light, just barely, and that's all I can recall.

Time passes, and I haven't thought of you for years, my strange friend. I'm far different looking here and now in this body than ever before. I know this because I saw reflections of my many selves in the mirror. I wonder if you know about this too? Although my image changes from one body to the next, I'm still me—even over the ages.

Nine years later in came a new encounter. I was in college taking general subjects and art classes. My professor wanted me to study under a master photographer because he'd never had a student advance so quickly. I imagined I'd end up working in NYC. My first love, David from high school, was touring the country as a musician. We'd headed in separate directions.

A new friend and I were starting to get serious. I'd fallen asleep at his house and was dreaming when a man came to see me. When I realized he was a vampire, I wasn't afraid because he was a good man— not a bloodsucker. He and I both became emotional when he pulled me to him, but I don't know the why of it. We held on to each other, and I wanted to stay there, but just as I was pushing back a little to look him in the eye, something started shaking me, which caused the vampire to turn into a coat hanger and fly away.

"Why did you wake me up?" I cried. My new boyfriend had interrupted the most important part of my dream.

"I heard you crying and moaning in your sleep," he said, gently massaging my shoulder. "When it woke me up, I was worried about you."

"Really? It wasn't a nightmare," I said, surprised that my dreams had disturbed someone else's sleep.

To this day, I know the man in my dream exists somewhere as a real person. It wasn't me embracing me—it was someone who was trying to reach me. I didn't explain that I do have actual visitors at times.

Nine months later, I received a long-distance proposal from this new boyfriend and moved to California. I put the vampire dream behind me, even though I knew this dream was more than just a dream. It was one of those real ones.

Three years later came an experience far different from the invisible day visitors who had given me information and guidance when I was four years old. Recurring dreams of going through doors had prepared me for specific doors that would open when they judged me ready.

A particular door opened when the night visitors came. I smelled my deceased mother, who returned to our realm to protect me from an immense force that had opened the door to initiate me. Although I was alone in my bedroom, it felt like I was outside in the elements. The atmosphere changed to a shuddering-shivering realm colder than the North Pole, and then the winds picked up and a storm came to deliver me into the eye of a hurricane.

It's a strange feeling to perceive the world in terms of consciousness coming in like an ocean. If you don't understand what I mean, it sounds irrational, but it isn't: my mother and this same immensity also visited my sister who lived two hundred miles away.

During the encounter, I managed to stay in the eye of this hurricane as information manifested like it came from invisible ink until what was drawn appeared in the outer world, written as actual events. At first, I discounted this scroll of information in disbelief—not like putting it on sale, or even offering it for sale. It's wisdom can't be bought, and its reality is above gold. No wonder the flies were everywhere. Was I ever innocent and ideal? The answer is yes because I'd forgotten everything I once knew about these realms.

As a child, I tried to open this powerful door many times in my dreams but was shooed away by my wiser guides. I am telling you this because I also saw a man during this experience and because I did not know him, I didn't know what make of his appearance at the time.

I'm nearing the reason why I decided I had to write to you. You'll see what I mean when I try to explain how I lead a normal life and a supernatural one at the same time. Although others want to make it their business, some things need to be kept secret.

Supersensitive testing wasn't part of my job at all when I was put into a trance at work and saw images of political and religious men along with whales, sharks, and a U-shaped power building representing destruction. Still standing in a trance, I kissed someone I love at a window, sliding down the glass with my lips staying attached like a suction cup all the way to the floor.

That was the day I was an unwitting guinea pig on the job. I left the job that very day, but it didn't even occur to me that it wasn't over—not at all. My field of energy had expanded due to the experimentation.

Just months earlier, I saw an unusual radiating light one night. It was the most exquisite, loving wonder I've ever seen and felt. It turned out to be an internal visitor—my boyfriend didn't experience it when we were making love. But for some reason, I wasn't the only one on earth to see it or feel it.

This phenomenon triggered me enough to see a psychic who was highly recommended. I'll get to that a little later in this letter. Thanks to my seeing that stunningly beautiful light, I met a man who had been looking all over for me. You may have to reach within to figure out why—wise guy.

Well, it turned out I'd already gotten some experience I didn't realize was practical preparation for the game and pursuit that followed. I've often been followed—even before I was old enough to drive. When I got my license, the tailing was done both by car and on foot. I learned to elude the chasers by cutting the car lights and driving in the dark like some moonshiner on the run. Other times, it helped to walk fast.

"Never go out without a male escort," my mother told me. That was easy for her to say with three brothers over six feet tall who did protect her.

"Don't worry. I'll just wear a hat so they'll think I'm a guy," I replied. *If she only knew how it is out here.*

Well, I guess all that chancy fox-hunt training paid off. When my intuition kept telling me an even odder chase was on, I finally had to accept the testing was because of my abilities.

"They're not supposed to be doing that," said a friend when I told him about my situation.

"Well, they are," I replied, wondering who the infamous "they" might be. I didn't know how to think about it.

But I recalled how when I was a teenager, a beautiful neighbor went through a weird, testing situation. Anonymous people decided to use her for some reason, and they put her on trial like she was a kind of guinea pig. She told me what they were doing and how they were doing it, and that's just what I was ignoring when similar people tried to get my attention with various communication devices. This is all I will say. By the way, I didn't think she was the one who was off her gourd.

In my situation, I did my own experimentation with my expanded awareness to get my bearings. I even stopped working for a while because a second agency job was no different.

An example of how I followed my nose was when I used my intuition to pick Telegraph Avenue in Berkeley, California, for an adventure and to experiment on my own. While walking along, I met an unusual young man. When we started talking, I learned his father could find anyone in the world using his abilities like a bloodhound. It was his dad's job to locate people using his special talent.

How Do I Know?

After he told me this, I didn't know if I'd found him or he'd found me. We talked about all kinds of weird things. When the subject turned to music, I named what I liked. "Yes!" he exclaimed, repeating some names excitedly.

Then he read me and was empathetic to the sadness in me because suddenly, his mouth twisted, and he was shaking mad as he looked up at the sky. "You dogs. She knows exactly what is going on," he said angrily.

A psychic's reading came to mind immediately. "You will be highly visible like you are in every lifetime," said this wise lady named Judy.

Thank you. This man was another powerful ally. I placed my hand over his heart to protect him because it felt so heavy, like it was mine. He didn't notice me shielding him because he was still looking skyward. He didn't need my problem, but he'd picked up on it immediately. It was obvious the son had inherited some of his father's gifts.

This stranger gave me his full name before saying, "If you ever need anything, come to Missouri." I'll find him by looking up an Argonaut and the smartest dog. I won't reveal his personal information, but I can tell you he was serious, and he meant what he said. At the time, I did wonder if I might have to take him up on his offer of help.

We walked to an Ethiopian restaurant for dinner, and afterward, I gave him a ride back to his hotel. Then we parted ways and never saw each other again.

You're probably wondering why I've even mentioned this event. It's because Judy understood what was going on. She told me, "Do not pay any attention to these dogs in the temple."

I didn't ask what she meant—dog clans, packs of dogs, dog men, or just plain dogs. I love dogs, but what are dog men? Was the psychic referring to what the American prophet Edgar Cayce called "the mixtures"?

Yes, the father of the man I met in Berkeley had the ability to track and locate like some dogs, but it didn't sound like he or his son misused their abilities. The way the son was able to perceive my situation was amazing, and I will never forget what he did.

Well, how many nosy people can tail along when you're on a high trail next to the Pacific Ocean? That's why I went for a hike in the Marin Headlands with a plan to find a place to read.

I needed shelter from more than the sun and saw a thicket ahead. It looked like an ideal shady spot to sit and read my book, *The Secret Teachings of All Ages* by Manly P. Hall. I crouched almost to my knees to get inside. It was a perfect circle of bushes and like being in a tent. I was about to sit down when I was hit by a terrible smell. I had to leave immediately because I had selected a pee hub and was overwhelmed by the odor of dog urine. It was like getting my own nose rubbed in a dog temple. Talk about reinforcing the psychic's advice to forget about them.

Please don't tell anyone about what's next. When you read on, you'll know exactly why.

Yes, my life changed after I was blindsided—tested for certain abilities on two jobs. I was still walking around with my large extended energy field thanks to being opened. As the stranger I met in Berkeley said, "It's like you've finally taken the blinders off."

A few days later, when I walked into a Larkspur Landing bookstore looking for a few books, I caught some guy peeking over the aisle at me before he ducked down completely. Although I wanted to run around to where he stood, I didn't. Right before the clerk rang me up, some nosy person in the back room wanted to see the books I was purchasing. I found it odd because this had never happened and besides, these weren't the last copies.

Those dogs again? I needed to forget about them, and they needed a restraining order.

In addition to getting these books, I was following a thread of energy that day, and that's why I walked along the scenic path to a particular area near the bay. I found it ended with a stranger—a coach for a boys' rowing team.

He stopped me and eyeballed me the way a coach does before speaking. "You are a Yugoslavian Olympic rower," he announced.

I kept my mouth shut. I was not. *Hmm. Is he kidding me?* I just stood there looking at him before deciding to play along.

"You can put your books and things in my car," he said, pointing to his VW. Then he turned and calmly headed toward the dock.

"Okay, thanks." I nodded and put everything in his car. The closer I got to the dock, the more I wondered if I'd just happened to show up before the real female rower.

Yes, the coach introduced me to the crew as a Yugoslavian Olympic rower. He grabbed his bullhorn before climbing into a catamaran next to the dock. Then he got to work.

The boys were already in the crew boat and ready to row. When I moved along the dock, getting closer to the empty seat, I noticed it had shoes built into the hull.

"Oh yes. Right." I giggled and did a little jump into the air with a few kicks before landing and dancing a few steps backward to get rid of my own shoes.

This situation was weird but intriguing. *Where is this going? Should I tell the coach before I get in the boat that he's mistaken me for another rower?* No, since I was curious, I decided not to blow the cover he gave. Besides, something else was going on.

I walked nimbly to the empty seat on the boat, which was for me. As I put my feet into the shoes and my hands on the pole in front of me, the coach yelled, "Starboard!"

Starboard, I thought to myself, looking into the dark green water for hints. I felt I should know the term, but I had no idea what part of the boat the coach was referring to—did it mean front, back, left, or right? *Well, here I am again, the only girl playing a sport with a crew of guys.*

After about a minute of trying, I couldn't row in sync. I had to give up and hold the oar right above the water so I wouldn't throw off everyone's rhythm. *I'm the Olympic rower, all right.*

Every time I saw their oars scoop the water, it was tempting to give it another try. But then I thought of canoeing for the first time. "I can paddle a canoe in a circle," I announced. This made the rowers chuckle. These were good-natured boys like the ones I've been around all my life, which I appreciated.

They knew I wasn't a rower. I just hoped I wasn't spoiling their practice altogether. I was having fun because being so close to the water without having to row is fantastic.

In no time, we neared the section of Larkspur Landing where old wood buildings look like a nineteenth-century ghost town. Around and above us were old, abandoned train tracks. One wooden pillar was like a track heading to the sky that ended abruptly like unfinished business. I thought of Sarah Winchester's infamous Mystery House mansion in San Jose, California, where stairs don't lead anywhere and doors open to nowhere.

We'd stopped in an area shaded by the overpass when an identical racing shell glided nearer, pausing when it was just parallel to our craft. The coach's catamaran was positioned in front of the two rows of boats, just where you'd find a teacher in a classroom.

I wasn't paying much attention to the boys in the other boat until the coach spoke to one of them. Using his bullhorn for all to hear, he asked the boy, "Is this your sister?"

The boy looked at me and I looked at him. We neither confirmed nor denied it. Maybe the coach had briefed him too. The boy didn't look surprised, but I was because he could have been your twin, Worse-A-Doodle. The likeness shocked me so much that I almost jumped out of the boat and into the water. He was a handsome boy who looked exactly like you. Even so, I wasn't going to say that out loud.

I don't know why this happened. For the entire summer, it seemed as though men were trying to point you out to me in various ways, while I was trying to protect you by remaining silent.

An odd thing happened days before the rowing experience. I was unmistakably push-guided to walk up to a door of an unknown house. It had your last name on the nameplate. Ha ha. No, I didn't knock. It is my feeling that I was pushed by good spirits like the ones who proved themselves when I was four. I think it was to let me know to keep your identity inside. That's why I said nothing to the rowing coach just to be safe and to keep you safe. That's how much you mean to me, my friend.

Maybe you were the male vampire character in my dream who was trying to pull me away from my former boyfriend. This is far-fetched, but if you had a dream where you were dressed as a vampire for Halloween and encountered an unfamiliar blond-haired, blue-green-golden-eyed female dressed in an all-black paper costume—that would have been me.

I have no doubt about this whatsoever now. You were the stranger who was there the night my deceased mother came back to visit me along with that powerful immensity. I thought your appearance in my experience was insane because it made no sense, but not anymore—not after your double showed up during my rowing adventure.

It wasn't always easy, but I continued to ignore the dogs in the temple when they'd say things and ask questions. "You have to tell us where you're going." "What's it going to take?" *What, the opening of my mouth?* Yes, doesn't this sound crazy? Well, there's more to all of it.

The psychic I keep mentioning gave me an unearthly reading

about my history and similar purpose for being here now. What she told me about energy is what I've been experimenting with on my own after it was ignited on my job. She also said, "You will meet your husband, but not in the normal sense."

Do you have any idea what she meant? I don't, but I may have gotten a whiff of it when I accidentally locked myself out of my own house after being out on another adventure.

I was sitting on my front porch waiting for my boyfriend to come home and let me in. He couldn't accept what was happening to me, and no matter how I tried to explain it, he didn't understand me. It felt like I was being pulled away from him in both worlds.

Being accidentally locked out of the house gave me time to contemplate what was meant by such a peculiar relationship. There was a stillness to every leaf and blade of grass in our woodsy yard. I closed my eyes and relaxed into this tranquil setting to partner with it.

This is when I sensed a gentle current resembling air and detected the barest scent of a man's cologne. I felt a presence approaching and opened my eyes, but I didn't see anyone, so I closed them again.

The movement of the current became stronger with a hint of weight, and the cologne's aroma became more intense as it billowed around me like a soft blanket. Although the sun was too bright for me to see without any sunglasses, I figured maybe my visitor was invisible.

Unafraid, I leaned back against my front door. The man exuded the soothing energy of a supportive and loving friend as he moved even closer. Although his cologne scent covered me through and through, I don't think this male was a freshly dead spirit. He could have projected himself in a trance, or he could have been a person in a body who was dreaming, but I don't know for sure.

Gustav Klimt's gorgeous painting *The Kiss* shows exactly how my encounter with the man on my porch felt. We had somehow merged, and I didn't want my visitor to ever leave or take his enveloping and expanding loving feeling away.

Is this what the psychic meant about meeting my husband, but not in the normal sense? I was determined to find out.

Sometimes, my curiosity gives the go-ahead. Not only did I want to see what the unusual future meeting meant, but I also didn't want to wait for it. I had to know right now, and I wanted it to be right now. Since my energy field was wide open, I tried to will it so by pushing ahead in the river of time or pulling the time to me.

This didn't fly too well. I had received some strong advice from this same psychic. She'd said, "Ground yourself. Are you trying to put future time into this time? You are causing a poltergeist effect in the atmosphere. It's like having the power of a nuclear bomb." Those were her exact words.

Yes, cry, cry, cry me a river. Love means everything to me. Now, I have to wait for time to catch up. There was a lot to learn or relearn before I was ready. Okay, so I've been attending the hard knocks school of enlightenment.

It'll help if I tell you about a few of my lessons. You'll see why dreams are more than nothing. Then you'll understand what I've learned about what "not in the normal sense" could mean.

In a dream, I asked my sister Helen and the old boyfriend who proposed to me long distance if they wanted to go to Egypt with me. They did. We were there in an instant, dressed as Egyptians and dancing at a large party.

After mingling and dancing, I was transported to black space and instantly to a temple chamber, where I found myself kneeling alone. At this height, my right arm was extended, and my fingers were skimming over the hieroglyphics I had no trouble reading.

Soon, my present mind caught up to this past me and I thought, *Diana, what are you doing? You don't know how to read hieroglyphics.* The moment I thought this, I was whisked into black space and then back to the party.

When it was time to go, I found myself alone in black space, and this time, I wanted to know where the edges of the universe were. So, I called out, "Ha!" The sound traveled out like something dropped in a finite body of water. When it hit the water's edges, it reverberated back, causing my entire body to vibrate like a bell. I felt like a fish flopping on land.

Startled, I woke up, still flopping, and when I tried to scream, nothing moved until I felt part of myself hit the mattress as I landed back into the rest of myself. I was on my back and still in my bed. That's when I knew I'd really been out after hours and had one wild trip home.

This adventure turned out to be a reality dream because when I called my sister and our mutual male friend, I discovered both had a dream about going to Egypt the night before. What would be the odds of that happening?

My dreams of being out in space are educational ones. For some reason, males have been my instructors or my companions every time. In fact, you might be the man with me here, Doodle. See if this sounds familiar to you.

Again, I was in the blackness of outer space, like it was a night out on the town, and I was calmly floating upright as though I was in a buoyant ocean. I was only there a short time before I heard a male voice say, "He's jealous. You have to move."

Move? I thought. "God, are you slow? I've already moved," I answered. I don't know about you, but I can talk to God or whoever it is like that because even though his voice is full of authority, he has a sense of humor.

I thought I was alone until I heard another male speak. "Well, God had to tell me three times," he said to me.

"Ha ha," I chuckled. This brotherly voice was nice and clear, and although I couldn't see its source, I knew he was close by. It was good to be there with someone like family who also floated in this outer-space ocean.

That's exactly as it happened. It may be a long shot, but did you hear any of this? Have you ever caught yourself in black space?

Now that I have your attention, the time has come for me to tell you what I'm sure you already know. I'm so grateful I've gotten all these visits from you. And I'm grateful that I was finally able to hear and see the real you, eye to eye in the normal sense after all this time. It's a relief to recognize each other on the outside too, like I knew we would.

Just knowing you believe what I've told you is very important to me. I understand if you didn't know what to think at first. I also had a hard time believing certain things about our relationship.

Now that I know you know me too, I'll mention how you were at it again. I was out one night under a string of city lights when I noticed you making your way down the main street where I live and heading my way.

I think you must enjoy surprising me. When we were close enough to run into each other, you showed me your teeth. It was almost like you said, "Boo." I was so startled that I screamed.

I mourned the loss of your pointy lateral incisors and wasn't prepared for your sudden reveal. Pay no attention to my preference for the unusual. Who am I to judge?

Well, what I assumed was just a teeth dream wasn't. It was reality. You didn't even have to scare me by biting me so that I'd get it. The next time I saw you smile, I noticed that you did have those exact dream teeth. Yes, my night visitor—you did. Did I pass that test?

It makes me happy to know I can say anything because nothing is too weird for you. You understand what I mean—what a relief. Sometimes, I don't have to say anything at all, but I do want to tell you, "Thank you."

Yes, it was a shock when I felt a ring go on my finger—and not in the normal sense. Do you know you kiss me a lot? I'm still getting used to your sneaking up on me. There is so much more to say than I can ever write here.

Someone once told me there are two cards missing from the tarot deck. It's taken me a long time to figure that one out. Thanks to you, I understand the mystery stories of Osiris and Isis and Solomon and Sheba.

The Lovers (Temple Brother and Sister) is a painting I created. It has "Song of Songs" written in Hebrew on the man's coat and on the woman's veil of life. When a woman visiting my art studio read the words, she said to me, "It's missing a hey."

I told her it was missing a "Hey you." She laughed at that.

Hey you. I miss you and I love you, but I know I'll see you soon.

Love,

Diana

PS: It only took us years to understand reality here—well maybe it took me years since I'm younger. We exist in different dimensions and time frames while the physics of the universe records us. I wish I'd known that as a wild teenager. Yes, call it a soul record or a life movie. It's like we're in some kind of time machine reality here.

There's something else important for you to know. It was just when I'd gotten into bed after turning out the lamp on my nightstand. The winter atmosphere in the room was chilly, so I pulled up the covers. When I'd gotten comfortable and settled in, I heard a male voice above me, just over my left eye.

How Do I Know?

"My dear, dear friend," you announced.

Although I was startled as usual, I smiled at the sound of your voice. *We must be going somewhere together.* I'm usually out a few minutes after my head touches the pillow, so I was surprised. I must have fallen asleep right after hearing myself say your name.

Racing to catch up to you, then flying straight up in the air, I caught myself awake in this dream. I even saw my feet push off from the pavement. Across the street there was an old, abandoned white car in a parking lot. Flying this way was exhilarating. You kept going and so did I, but the part of me still attached to my body had to come back.

Now I know why you kept going. You had already dropped your body, abandoning it like the old white car parked near my house. I should have known after seeing someone covered in plastic like a mummy wrapped up that it meant death. Maybe I received this information symbolically in my dream because my human part didn't want to face it.

You made the rounds like my mother did. She separated from her body shortly before she visited, and we detected its odor still attached to her. The official news of her death came a few hours later.

The next day, when my friend Barbara came to visit, we read the official news of your death. You must have made your final rounds days earlier. I'm honored to be the last person you came to visit. I love that we had a chance to see each other once more before you moved on.

After the shock and grief, I know you're gone, but you aren't gone altogether. We can communicate like before. You still visit and kiss my lips from time to time—just in a different form.

THE END

www.ingramcontent.com/pod-product-compliance
Lightning Source LLC
LaVergne TN
LVHW051225080426
835513LV00016B/1414